Dedication

I dedicate this book to the best friend a person could ever dream of, my husband Ron.
(Two computers going strong for two years!) Thanks for believing in me.
Also to my amazing children, better known as the test team and marketing division of <u>Life's on Fire</u>.
I would have hand picked every one of you all over again. I love you all.

Foreword

So many of us have such busy schedules trying to balance our family, career, social and spiritual lives, that these days something just has to give. In my case the give is cooking. It is a chore that I dread. It always results in last minute planning, racking my brain for something healthy, but quick.

For several years I have been fortunate enough to be working with what I'm passionate about; teaching people about choice, balance and boundaries required to create and maintain healthy relationships. Imagine my surprise at discovering that Sandi's passion is to teach people about healthy choices, balance and boundaries in the kitchen. Needless to say we are a match made in heaven.

When Sandi approached me to take part in testing recipes and weekly menus, I admit, I didn't quite believe this book could solve my mealtime dilemma. After all, I was preparing one meal for the adults, and scrambling to appease two small children with fussy palates, including a five year old self proclaimed vegetarian. Mealtime needed fixing. It was a nightmare to put it mildly!!

As I proceeded to do my first test week, I was amazed at the ease of using Sandi's system. It taught me to create boundaries in the kitchen with a simple timer. The children soon learned that "their time" is after prep time. As long as the timer is ticking, Mom or Dad can't be interrupted. We even began the "one bite rule" as Sandi suggests. To my surprise and theirs, they actually like most of the new foods and even ask for more!!

I soon discovered this is not your average cookbook. First of all, the recipes actually work, and they are delicious!! This is a weekly planner if I want it to be. It is a nutritional guide that helps me monitor my fat intake, plus, it is all bundled up in a time saving visual package! This is the book parents everywhere, including myself, have been praying for!! This system has changed the entire dynamics of mealtime in our home!

Kim S. Wall

Kim Wall
Success Unlimited
E-Mail: newknowledge@hotmail.com

Kim Wall

Kim is a Voice Dialogue Facilitator and Personal Growth Consultant. She specializes in the areas of communication, relationships, setting personal boundaries and self esteem.

Kim has studied under Hal Stone Phd. and Sidra Stone Phd., the developers of Voice Dialogue and authors of <u>Embracing Each Other</u>, and also Shakti Gawain, author of <u>Creative Visualization</u>.

She has been happily married for 10 years, has two daughters and currently resides in St. Albert, Alberta, where she leads workshops and does private consultations.

Table of Contents

Grocery Lists

The Relationship Between STRESS, SPEED, TASTE, and FOOD

STRESS

One morning I am in my doctor's office when an article catches my attention. A psychologist claims that supper time is in fact the most mind consuming and **STRESSFUL** part of a person's day!!! Oh, I think, all those people just need to get a life!! As I read on I realize **I need to get a life!!!** Scanning each line, I begin to daydream about my own family.

"What do you guys want for supper tomorrow?" Yikes, it starts the night before. I am worse than I thought!!

"Let's have curried chicken, Mom."

"Chicken wasn't on sale this week, we don't have chicken."

"What about tangy chops?"

"Hey, good idea.... nooope, I used the last bit of ketchup yesterday. I'll have to stop at the grocery store after work. Wait a minute, I can't stop at the grocery store. Doug has basketball as soon as I get home."

While continuing to scan the article, I see myself lying in bed thinking about what I can take out, then talking myself into putting the decision off until the next day, before work! Yeah right, and that's going to happen! There I am in the morning, solving problems, getting ready, rushing kids out the door, signing last minute papers, etc, etc, etc.

Guess what the main topic at work is that day? You got it! What am I going to make for supper!!! While sweat collects on my forehead, reviewing my insane schedule, I notice the same sick look on my co-workers faces. As I slip out of the daydream, I feel the panic set in and I think to myself, *"This psychologist guy has been to my house."*

That day changed everything for me. I cannot believe how much time is spent worrying about what I am going to have for supper.

SPEED

Ok! The first line of action, **SPEED**. Cooking takes time. How can I cut down the time? I found myself in the same old rut, picking the same meals over and over again. Why? Because I knew them off by heart. I love to cook, but follow a recipe after work? I don't think so!

I would scan uuuuup to the ingredients, doooown to the instructions, uuuuup to the ingredients, doooown to the instructions. - Where am I again? That's IT!!! I'm ordering pizza!! Oooor, dumping something onto a cookie sheet from a box! *"That's ok! We ate healthy last night!"*

Sooound familiar? I solved the problem. I rewrote my recipes the way I read, **left to right**. It helps! No more scanning up and down for this girl!!

Reading recipes left to right isn't enough. Most things just take too long to cook. I still need to cut the time down. I have an idea! I combine my favorite spaghetti sauce from a jar with fresh ingredients, to make what I think is one darn good sauce. Why not see what else is out there! The mission begins. It becomes a game, a hobby, an obsession. I am going to beat this thing.

I **sourced products** that were ahead of their time on **health issues**. I tried to find products that had as **few preservatives as possible**. I would begin with an old recipe that we loved and replace components that would speed up the prep time.

Read on or don't complain about suffering...

I bought a **timer**. If I couldn't beat 20 minutes prepping, it didn't fit my life during the work week. Don't get me wrong, I still like to cut and chop and try new recipes on the weekend when my patience for failure is at a much higher level, **but not during the week**.

I picked what I would make for the week and made sure all the groceries were in the house. My recipes were now simple to read, they were fast to prepare...all was in place. Fooor a while....until....my kids started getting older and getting into more activities. My work started getting busier, more meetings in the evenings, youch!! I needed to adjust things.

I began **color coding** all of my recipes according to preparation and cooking times. Anything marked **red** or **yellow** means on the table **in less than 30 minutes**. The superduper fast ones get little wings. Sick huh!! (I was desperate, what can I say!!) The **green** and **blue** markings mean I have a small window of opportunity to come home, throw everything in the oven, then **tear off for an hour** while my magic oven does the rest!!

TASTE

People started calling. *"I heard you have a speedy gourmet stew that's to die for. Can I have the recipe?"* To die for is the key phrase here. If food doesn't **TASTE** great, people get turned off. It became ridiculous, people would give me their entertainment schedules begging for ideas. I began photocopying recipes to keep up with the demand. A survival system and everyone I knew wanted to have it! Being a mother of seven children these days is an organizational nightmare in itself. Buuut I never worry about supper.
I LIVE THIS BOOK!!!

FOOD

You want to know what I think about **FOOD** now, don't you? Do I care about today's research on food, fat content, etc? Well indeed I do, so let's talk about that! Food these days is the most confusing thing to figure out. We are plowed down by new facts on cancer fighting foods, heart attack prevention foods, eating for your personality foods. Oh, this one kills me... **All the animals in the animal kingdom have been weaned off their mother's milk within 6 weeks. We don't need milk!!** Reeeeally!! Well until I see a cat, dog or cow making major corporate decisions or running a country, I'll opt for a modern **balanced diet**.

Don't get me wrong (and please note this is only my lowly opinion), I think almost every new fad diet starts with some really great research. In fact I think it's neat looking into that research, but here's a guideline: If you have children it's your job to feed them a balanced diet for proper bone and brain development. As an adult you can make your own choices, but ask yourself three important questions.

Do I have the time?
Do I have the money?
Do I have the self discipline?

These are very important questions because our intentions for being healthy are all in the right place. If you don't have the **time** to cater to your adult beliefs while providing your children with what they need, you're going to find it very stressful. Can you support the theory **financially**? Do you need to supplement with expensive vitamins to make up for the missing components? Will you get frustrated because you're hungry and **justify extra snacks**.

The **Canadian and American Food Guides** have been revised to reflect more recent studies. A ton of research goes into these guides. They have analyzed new information and adjusted fat intake (for heart), fruits and vegetables (for cancer) and they balance your diet in a way that you are not left hungry.

My survival system has **nutritional information data**, including **food choice** exchanges, right in front of your face, for the whole meal. You will see what a health nut I really am! Look closely at some of the low-fat cookbooks. <u>Do your own homework</u>. Ask yourself; *"This recipe has only 8 grams of fat, can I live on 1/2 a chicken breast without snacking tonight?"* Have they included the rice, or the pasta, or the vegetables. I must now add up all the components, including how much chicken I'm reeeeally going to eat, and **then** calculate the fat.

TEST FAMILIES

We had to beg 16 different families to help test the system. *"Ah, I can't commit to that, I'm too stressed out as it is,"* was the most common phrase!! We felt like a burr in our friends, co-workers, and friends of friends sides. (That's when our friends pawned us off on some unwilling soul, just to get rid of us!) They had to take a given week, make the five recipes in a seven day period and return them to us with their comments and their ratings. Not even we expected the results we received. The average week rated 4.5 out of 5. In fact, we got a lot of calls saying things like, *"I don't believe you gave me a selected week! Prove it to me. I think these are your favorites! I want another week!!"* (Thanks for thinking we're big liars, Rob!!) After the second week, the phone rang off the hook from people who now wanted to test the recipes. By the time we were done with our data and were satisfied it wasn't just our family who **loved the food**, we closed testing! The very same people who were stressed out about testing, were now stressed out that we were no longer testing!

RESULTS

I was once told by a very reputable person (who deals with food and publishing) that the average national best selling cookbook has very few recipes that you may repeat on a regular basis. If that's the case, you're going to fall over with the results from this book. These recipes pass our family's taste tests and they have passed the taste tests of 16 other different types of families. They have passed the taste tests of cooking classes we conducted (which resulted in learning about buying habits) and they have passed the taste tests of approx 120 different families which we fed alternately over the past 3 years! We certainly did our homework!!

The photography is real. It drives me nuts when I make something, and there is noooooo way it looks anything like the picture, and I can cook. I can't imagine the poor souls who are just learning how to cook. They probably get turned off for life!!! We used **no shaving cream, no glycerin not even a single blow torch!!** We cooked the food and had a photographer take pictures of the actual food!! Go figure!!

It's a real high for me when I can help someone to understand that cooking during the week can actually be low stress. I know that's what you'll discover with my book!! Enjoy!!

A Different Way of Thinking
= SPEED

...and health for life

My Food Beliefs

If nutritious food can't be fast, you may eat something you shouldn't.

Calories from fat should not exceed **30%** of your total caloric intake on a daily basis.

Frozen vegetables may be healthier than fresh! Wow, that's a big one!! Food manufacturers have the capability to remove some of the harmful chemicals off vegetables by washing, in a much more advanced way than we can in our home. Think about it!! There's a time to use fresh, when you have time to remove the chemicals properly. Let someone else do the work when you're in a rush.

Meats should be **trimmed**, so purchase them that way. You don't have time. Boneless, skinless chicken is best! Don't tell yourself you can't afford it, tell yourself you need that help for cooking quickly. Besides, are you really saving money when buying untrimmed or cheaper cuts? When I buy a 750 g pkg of untrimmed steak, I end up with 500 g and worse, it takes me extra time I don't have!

Carbohydrates are **essential** for energy. Dry pasta, rice and potatoes are great for storage and have a high rate of success. Use different varieties of pasta and rice to make meals more interesting. It's okay to buy dehydrated potato flakes, canned potatoes or dehydrated potato slices. If you don't consider speed, what's the alternative?

If you have kids, **you are not running a restaurant**. You need to provide them with a protein, a carbohydrate and a fruit or vegetable at supper.
Some will be meat eaters and some will be vegetarians. Most will like the carbohydrate. Make a rule that they **must** have a very small **taste** of the part they hate. Don't make them gag, just introduce it. Suggest they down it with milk, plug their nose, or do whatever it takes. This introduces different flavors into their palate and eventually eliminates stress for you! Don't let them snack if they don't eat the part they usually like. This is your stamp of approval for poor eating habits!!

Buying your **groceries in advance** saves you money, that's why we provided you with **rip out grocery lists**. We also provided you with custom lists where you can fill in the blanks. If you don't like the way our weeks are set up, go ahead and set up your own. One of the most frequent comments we received from the test families was, *"I don't get it. I'm buying helpers and better quality meats but my grocery bill has gone down."* Do you know why??? I don't know about you but it costs me 25 bucks every time I go into a store to buy a loaf of bread!!! If your groceries are all ready for you, you'll **save money,** because you don't need to be walking into a store every second day. Think about that!!

3 Steps
Will Keep You Healthy and Stress Free

Step 1

Take your grocery list to the store.

Step 2

Choose your color according to the insanity of your life that night.

Step 3

When taking out what you'll need BEFORE YOU GO TO WORK glance to the left of the clock to check the grams of fat for supper. Adjust your fat intake during the day!

4 Steps
Will Change Your Attitude About Weekday Cooking

Step 1

Put on your apron over your daytime clothes.
(work isn't over until the work is over)

Step 2

Take out ingredients.
(beginning the task takes most of the thinking)

Step 3

Take out equipment.
(it's like working out, it's not the exercise I hate, ... but getting there)

Step 4

Set your timer to set your boundaries.
(there is now a real beginning - more importantly, ... a real end)

Congratulations...
These are the first steps to being and feeling healthy.

A Different Way of Doing Things
When You Looove Food

The cooking classes I held and the test weeks that were conducted helped me understand what people generally liked to eat, what their buying patterns were and how they did things in the kitchen. They loved my recipes, so that part was great, however, the other two pieces of information I gathered were quite surprising.

Canadians (generally) **purchase in metric**...and...**measure in Imperial**. **WOW!!!**
I made the mistake of producing my grocery lists using Imperial. People, mostly quite well educated people I might add, would ask, *"The list says 1-1/2 pounds boneless, skinless, chicken thighs...That's about 700 grams, right?"* Oh No! I misread my Canadian buyer. They're modern, they're metric! I quickly do my conversions in my head as I continue to instruct by saying, *"It's now time to put 5 mL of curry powder in with your meat."* *"Is that a teaspoon?"* someone asked. My goodness! That's exactly how I think! Anything I purchase is in metric, but my mom taught me to cook with an Imperial measure. I have written all the recipes out this way. For those who have done the complete switch, I also provide a conversion chart. When the cover is opened out pops the conversion chart, no matter what recipe you're on! That is my brilliant mother-in-law's idea. Thanks mom!!!

Being stubborn has no place in a modern kitchen

(Or...... stop your complaining about hating to cook.) **Take rice for example... Yes, lets!**

If you say, *"I don't cook my rice in the microwave. I only like it cooked on the stove,"* then you have no reason to whine!!! Cook things so they are ready at the same time. If the meal is cooking in the oven for about an hour, throw your rice in beside it. If you are fussing with things on the stove, you may want to cook it in the microwave. If you are using your microwave, you may want to cook it on the stove. Be flexible to change. You will not believe how much stress this actually eliminates!

Why some prepared products may be a healthier choice during the work week

When I began the test weeks I was very surprised at how people viewed prepared products. They said things like...*"Can I just peel my own potatoes instead of buying canned potatoes?"* *"Well of course you can, I'm not your mother!!! For the success of the test weeks, however, you need to do the recipes exactly the way you receive them and it's those kinds of comments we are looking for."* I secretly knew they would come back and say: *"Wow!! Those things are great! I can't believe I've never used these before!!"* Aaaand they did. You see, we guilt ourselves into thinking that we can do it all, so we try.

I then asked people, *"Do you ever buy frozen deep fried prepared food?"* *"Well yea!! Only as a back-up."* Interesting isn't it! North Americans have convinced themselves that it's okay to cheat completely when it's really bad for you, but you shouldn't kinda cheat with the pretty healthy stuff.

WHO MADE THIS PLAN?... AND... WHY ARE WE FOLLOWING IT?
I suggest it's because we are constantly being sent mixed messages. We are being pelleted with reports on fat and sodium content - but where are the reports on the foods we're using in a pinch? ...and we do. The latest statistics on sales of prepackaged deep fried food in boxes tells us we are drastically failing at pulling off a healthy supper during the work week.

Terrific Helpers

There are some pretty terrific helpers out there, just waiting for you to appreciate them.
I approached the companies you see listed on this page. **There is no financial compensation for using their names**, in fact it's quite a bit of red tape to have permission to use their names. Do you know why? **They needed to check me out** to make sure I didn't make them look bad - go figure! I really believe in them. There are many other great products out there, but these are some of my personal favorites. The following product and company names appearing in this book, in the recipes and in the grocery lists, are trademarks or trade names of their respective companies.

PILLSBURY, GREEN GIANT and SWEETLETS are registered trademarks of The Pillsbury Company; PILLSBURY JUMBO CRESCENTS, PILLSBURY COUNTRY BISCUITS, GREEN GIANT JAPANESE STYLE, GREEN GIANT CALIFORNIA STYLE and GREEN GIANT ORIENTAL STYLE are trademarks of The Pillsbury Company. OLD EL PASO is a registered trademark of Pet. Incorporated.

CATELLI®, CATELLI BISTRO®, CATELLI EXPRESS®, GARDEN SELECT®, HEALTHY HARVEST® and CATELLI and rainbow design® are registered trademarks owned by BF Foods International Corporation and CATELLI GARDEN SELECT and CATELLI HEALTHY HARVEST are trademarks owned by BF Foods International Corporation.

*Reg'd T.M. of Alberto-Culver Co.

Uncle Ben's ® Converted ® Brand Rice, Uncle Ben's ® Brand Brown Rice, Uncle Ben's ® Brand Basmati Rice, Uncle Ben's Classics ™ Oriental Spring Vegetable Rice, Uncle Ben's ® Fast & Fancy ® Mushroom Rice, Uncle Ben's ® Stuff'N Such Traditional Sage are registered Trademarks of EFFEM Inc. © EFFEM INC.

Campbell's Bisto

Reg'd T.M. of
Campbell Soup Company Ltd.

Reg'd T.M. of
McCain Foods Limited

VH Foods

Reg'd T.M. of
V-H Foods

Different Colors - WHY?

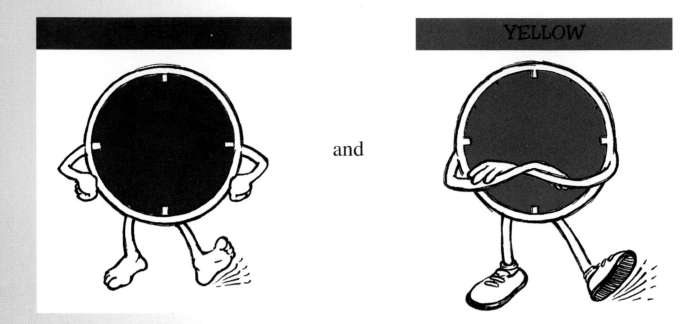

and

Eating time is **30 minutes** for the days you need to get your butt out of the house fast.

 If either Red or Yellow have Wings, eating time is 25 minutes

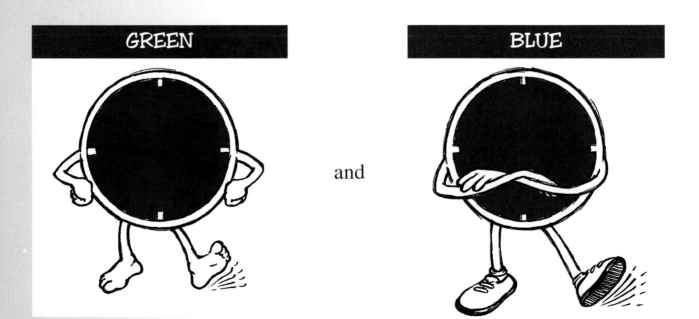

and

You have a small window of opportunity to prepare, but need to rush off somewhere before you eat. Eating time is **60 minutes**.

Color Coding
How it will Save Your Life

Flip through the pages and you will notice that all the photography and clocks are in the color relating to the speed of the dish.

It's this easy

Red

- You need supper on the table in 30 minutes
- <u>Less</u> cutting and chopping

Yellow

- You need supper on the table in 30 minutes
- <u>More</u> cutting and chopping

Green

- For the nights when you have a window of opportunity to prepare, but everything gets tucked away to cook on it's own for 40-60 minutes
- <u>Less</u> cutting and chopping

Blue

- For the nights when you have a window of opportunity to prepare, but everything gets tucked away to cook on it's own for 40-60 minutes
- <u>More</u> cutting and chopping

Red or Yellow Wings = on the table in 25 minutes

Each week has either 2 Reds and a Yellow **or** 2 Yellows and a Red
Each week has at least one Wings dish

This is my life this week;

You have bought your groceries, you look over your week.

Monday:	Meeting at 6 •••••••	**Red or Yellow with Wings**
Tuesday:	I'm home for 1/2 hour and then my daughter has hockey •••	**Green**
Wednesday:	Other daughter has dancing at 7 •••••••	**Red or Yellow**
Thursday:	Home for a bit, must pick son up from school after volleyball •••	**Blue**
Friday:	Get kids off to the movies with their friends •••••••	**Red or Yellow**

Step 1: Use pre-printed or custom grocery list.
Step 2: Choose color of supper according to the insanity of your life that night.
Step 3: When you take out the stuff you'll need (before you go to work) look to the left of the clock - find out the fat content for supper and adjust your fat intake during the day!

What These Symbols Mean?

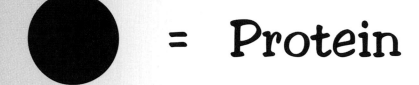 = Protein

 = Vegetable

■ = Carbohydrate

How do the symbols on the left of the recipe work and what on earth do they mean?

● **Red circle = some type of protein**

■ **Blue square = some type of carbohydrate**

▲ **Green triangle = some type of fruit or vegetable**

Why?

We are not accustomed to reading a recipe that gives you all the components of a meal. It's usually only one component. These symbols help you breeze through each step with a clear indication of which part of the meal you are working on.

My test week families like these symbols for another reason!
When a person is miraculously free on the weekend for a while (which is clearly some strange phenomenon), they sickeningly choose to freeze ahead some meals in their spare time. (They're only my friends, I'm not related.)
They choose their favorite freezer type meals, make up their own grocery list and follow the main course symbols only. Then when they pull them out during the week they follow the recipe to fill in the missing components. (eg. salad, pasta, etc...)

The symbols are very useful for <u>adults</u> who have adopted a belief in food research, but need to provide their children with a balanced diet until they are old enough to apply their own beliefs.

Make the whole meal, however:

• If you believe in eating mostly meats with fruits and vegetables:
  Serve yourself the red circle and the green triangle.

• If you believe you should combine a vegetable with a meat or a carbohydrate but not both:
  Serve yourself the green triangle with one of the others.

• If you believe that meat is not good for your body:
  Serve yourself the blue square with the green triangle. (This doesn't however always make for a very interesting vegetarian meal, but it will help in a rush.)

For rushed individuals <u>without</u> children.
Do whatever your little heart desires and you can use the symbols to cater to your own beliefs.

Note: If you are vegetarian, the celery huggers displayed on each week's intro page indicate a great meal with tofu, plain veggies, or soya replacement for ground beef.

Cutting for Speed

No fancy schmancy in the work week

How to cut an onion

trim ends, toss out:

cut in half:

peel:

follow the grain:

How to cut a mushroom

trim end, toss out

cut:

lie on flat side:

How to cut a roast beef for one hour cooking

flip over:

fat side down, make ½ inch Slices, ¾ of the the way down:

grab and flip back over:

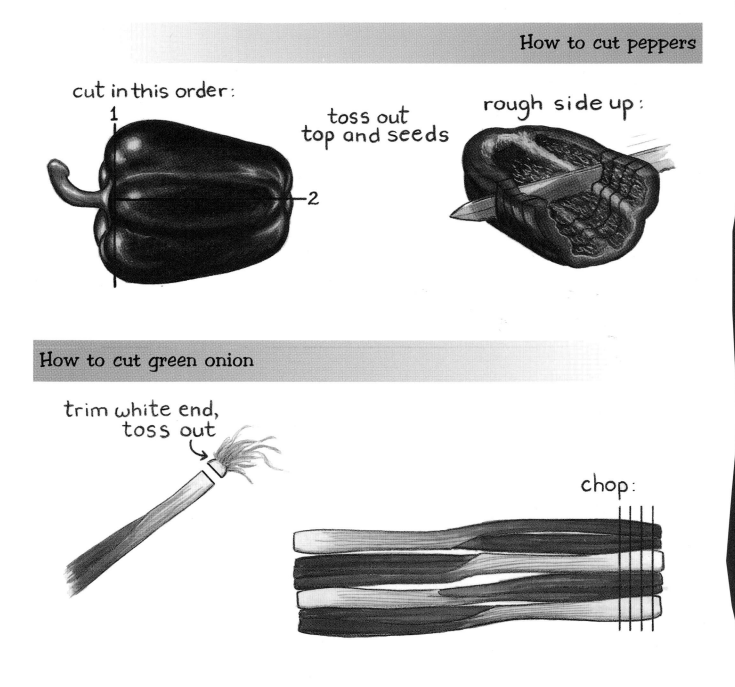

cut in this order:
1
2

toss out
top and seeds

rough side up:

How to cut green onion

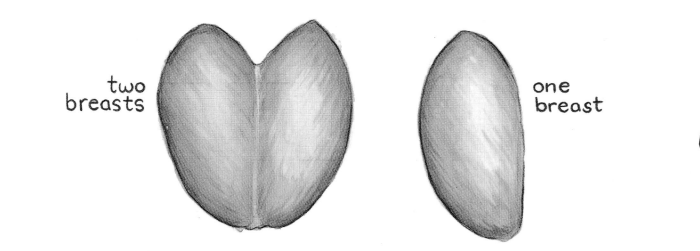

trim white end,
toss out

chop:

There are two different ways you may find chicken breast sold at stores

two
breasts

one
breast

You Must Own

Apron

If you don't have one, buy one....a full length one. There is some strange relationship between **changing into your jeans and not making supper**. If you really want work to end, end your work before you change!!

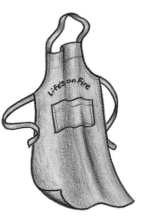

Cutting Board

Make sure you have a good cutting board that doesn't slip and is easy to pick up. Remember, it's to dump the stuff you're cutting into the pan. I call it my easy food transferer. It's a bonus that it protects my counters. (That's okay! I also call my dishwasher the dish-hider. It's a bonus that it washes the dishes.)

Sharp Knives

We all would love to be able to afford sharp knives of great quality. I slowly purchased mine one at a time and gulped when I paid the price. There was, however, a temporary fix when I couldn't even afford to buy one at a time. Buy knives that have sharpening holders. If you have dull meat and vegetable knives, it's one more excuse to give up, and **we all know, we're looking for any excuse we can get!**

Salad Spinner

They are only a few bucks. Watch for a deal, it's an invaluable time saving investment.

Large Oven and Microwave-Safe Pot for Rice

Our test families said, *"I never cook rice in the oven."* I said, *"You have to test the recipes the way we've written them or you can't have the recipes, na na na na na na!!"* Sometimes rice should be cooked on the stove, sometimes in the microwave and sometimes in the oven. It's all a matter of low stress and timing!

Timer

The best investment I ever made for lowering stress at supper time is an electronic timer. **It's for timing you**, not the food. **When you time yourself** during the work week there is a **real beginning** and more importantly a **real end**. I say to my family, *"I've taken my stuff out and I'm setting the timer."* My family knows that means DO NOT DISTURB. The test families said things like, *"I don't need a timer, I have lots of timers. One on the stove, one on the microwave, etc..."* From those who purchased a timer I got squealing messages left on the voice mail saying things like, *"This is so neat, it really works, even if I don't beat the timer the first time I try a recipe. It psychologically tells me, I'm done soon."* Try it you'll like it!!

Our Guidelines for Selecting Ingredients

Vegetables and fruits are medium size unless otherwise specified.
Herbs and spices are dry. You can purchase dried herbs two ways - ground or leaves. We use leaves unless otherwise specified.
We use extra virgin olive oil.

Calculating Nutritional Data

When a range is given for the number of servings a recipe makes, the higher number is used (eg. 4-6 servings - data is supplied for 6 servings, including food choices). We chose the suggested serving sizes. Our test families varied in size. Some people said there was way too much food for 4 people, some thought it was just right. If you have 4 adults in your home with very healthy appetites the recipe will probably serve 4. Here's an easy way to change the data. The formula works for calories, proteins, carbohydrates and fats.

Recipes Serving 4-6

# of g fat x 3 ÷ 2 = # of g fat for 4 servings

eg. 12 g fat x 3 = 36 divided by 2 = 18 g fat

(12 g fat per serving for 6 servings) = (18 g fat per serving for 4 servings)

Write this new information right on the recipe. Cross out the old and put in the new. Remember this is the way to monitor your fat intake for the day. You need the proper information. Mark the book, just like you would a daytimer. That's why we chose this type of binding. Feel great about staying on top of your health.

Produce

Head of lettuce or bunch of spinach has
    7-1/2 cups edible leaves (216 g)
    large... 10 cups edible leaves (288 g)
    small ... 3.75 cups edible leaves (108 g)

Onion	180 g
small	120 g
large	240 g
Roma tomato	80 g
Potato - large	250 g
Pepper - red or green	200 g
small	125 g
Zucchini	210 g
small	125 g
Broccoli floweret - small	50 g
Apple	150 g

Baking Goods

French loaf	450 g
Baguette	350 g
Croissant - large	57 g
Bun	60 g
Multigrain bun	45 g
Dinner roll	30 g
Bread stick	20 g

Weights and Measures

- When a choice of two ingredients are listed (eg. blueberries or cranberries), the first ingredient is used for the data.
- Ingredients listed as optional are not included in nutritional data.
- Rice has no butter added even when instructions on package suggest to do so.
- Dry scalloped potato mixes are 166 g with **half** the suggested butter added.
- Instant mashed potato flakes use **half** the suggested butter.
- When using cooking spray we assume a 3 second spray.

Dairy

Low-fat Cheddar cheese	6 % mf
Low-fat Monterey Jack cheese	17 % mf
Parmesan cheese	17 % mf
Swiss cheese	17 % mf

Frozen

Pie crust - lower-fat deep dish	180 g

Equipment List

When we say, "Don't change yet! Take out equipment." on the recipe, we're referring to don't change your work clothes. It's amazing how following this advice will reduce your stress.

Equipment List:
Lge oven-safe pot w/lid
Small microwave-safe pot w/lid
Rectangular lasagna or cake pan
Mixing bowl
Cutting board
Colander
Sharp veggie knife
2 lge mixing spoons
Measuring cups & spoons

Per serving:

Calories	436
Fat	6.4 g
Protein	32.4 g
Carbohydrate	62.2 g

Food Choices:

2	Starch
1 1/2	Fruits + Veg
0	Milk 1%
1/2	Sugars
3	Protein
2	Fat
0	Extras

Prep Time

Food Analysis

If you flip through the book, you will notice all the food data is displayed clearly on the top right hand corner near the clock which indicates speed. This is designed so that you can immediately see your fat intake for the meal you've chosen for supper. It tells you at the beginning of the day what you should be eating during the day.

Eg: If supper has 4 grams of fat and you know your daily fat intake should be 67 grams (based on a 2000 calorie intake), then you know you have 63 grams to play with during the day. That's a lot. If you know, on the other hand, your supper is 26 grams of fat (our highest) you have to watch your fat intake a little more closely during the day. This keeps you balanced, always!

Diabetic Food Choices and Why!

Because a very large number of people have some form of diabetes, we feel it is just as important to include this information as it is detailed nutritional analysis. Our recipes have very high standards for taste, speed and nutrition. It seems only fair to allow a person with diabetes the luxury of being able to use a regular cookbook with great tasting meals. They can simply adjust components according to their specific dietary requirements.

There is another very important reason for having food choices. Some people use food choices rather than traditional food analysis to monitor weight gain.

Marcia Lee

Marcia Lee was our on call Diabetes Food Choice Consultant. She mulled over and inputted page upon page of data (as Ron weighed almost every food item in the book). Thanks for your attention to detail, Marcia!

Marcia graduated as a registered nurse from the Foothills Hospital School of Nursing at the University of Calgary in 1979 and has worked as an ER nurse for 18 of the last 20 years. She has been an insulin dependent diabetic since the age of six. Her knowledge and attention to diabetes control with diet and insulin has enabled her to live an extremely active lifestyle, including becoming a certified scuba diver 8 years ago (having since logged over 100 dives).

Health   Sante
Canada   Canada

CANADA'S
Food Guide

TO HEALTHY EATING
FOR PEOPLE FOUR YEARS AND OVER

Enjoy a variety of foods from each group every day.

Choose lower-fat foods more often.

Grain Products
Choose whole grain and enriched products more often.

Vegetables and Fruit
Chose dark green and orange vegatables and orange fruit more often.

Milk Products
Choose lower-fat milk products more often.

Meat and Alternatives
Chose leaner meats, poultry and fish as well as dried peas, beans and lentils more often.

Canada

For Families with Older Children
or
Couples Who Are Bugged that the Other Partner Never Participates in the Kitchen

If both people work (this includes the volunteer selfless job of raising children), both people need to help out in the kitchen. (Just my lowly point of view speaking again.)

There are certainly exceptions to this rule:
Sometimes my husband and I agree that one will take over one responsibility, while the other takes over the meal. If it's agreed, everyone feels great!
Some people love to do all the cooking! Great!!

We saw something very interesting while doing our testing; nonparticipating partners were participating chefs. Why? We think it's because the thinking about what to make was eliminated coupled with trying a new adventure! We received a lot of feedback from people who said their relationship most definitely improved. Of all the highs in doing this book and sharing my family's survival system, those moments were the highest.

Older kids like to cook, even if they're lazy! Our kids and their friends are so proud when I make them try a recipe. They're so proud!! I'll never forget the night when Brandon and Cory (two of our daughter's friends) cooked dinner for our family. They wanted to test a recipe. I told them how the recipes read and how they had to take out all their stuff first and then set their timer. They couldn't believe how fast it took (szechuan orange-ginger chicken page# 148) *"I made this."* They kept saying, *"I can't believe it!"* There was, however, one slight problem in that Cory accidentally put the equivalent of 6 tsp hot garlic-chili sauce in, as opposed to the required 2-1/2 tsp. Ron, the kids and I loved it, because we don't mind spicy food, but poor Brandon and Cory drank about 15 L of water, huffing and puffing, as we howled! We kept saying, *"Hey, don't eat it!"* Guess what they said?
*"No way, **it tastes great**, it's just reeealy hot, **but we made it,** we're eating it!"* They were proud!
(We just don't let Cory loose with the chili sauce anymore.)

Do me a favor, ...no, do yourself a favor.
If you have purchased this book (of course you have, you're reading this) and you only plan on using it for recipes, not as a planner, great, you'll love the success for that reason alone. Buuuut we challenge you to try one grocery list, juuust once, for one week, any week. You will probably never go back!!

Be healthy.

Some Comments From Our Test Families

Love the fact that you throw everything in the oven at the same time. I enjoy choosing the blue and green dishes during the week because of that. Hands free and YUM!!

- John and Kim Wall

I love that grocery list! I felt like I really had my act together for meal planning (and I never feel like I have my act together for meal planning). I also loved the success of the recipes, we loved them all!

- Geralyn and Dan Rouault

We aren't zucchini fans but your Zucchini Parmesan was a pleasant surprise! Now another favorite!

- Denise and Gary Truhn

The recipes are so easy to understand that our older children enjoy making them. We love the flavors. I need this book!

- Jocelyn and Kelly Hansen

Family favorites every time! I can't believe how much we enjoy every recipe! I own a lot of cookbooks but my prize possession is my book of test recipes!! Get this book published!

- Rose and Gaston Monai

At first we didn't believe you gave us a specific test week. How could one week have this many great suppers! We're hooked! We were also surprised about the use of different spices, we didn't think we'd like some. What a great surprise!!

- Ann and Rob Campbell

✔ **This is a workbook. Write in it! It will look like mine after a while with little splat marks all over it!**

✔ **The rating space is not for decoration. Write in your family rating for future reference.**

✔ **Change the grams of fat data according to how many servings your family eats. (see page 24) This is an easy way to monitor your fat intake, daily.**

✔ **You may want to use this book just for the great recipes! If so, you're in for a big treat! But ... I challenge you - try one grocery list for one week, any week - and watch your stress level drop!**

Recipes

Things You Should Know About the Recipes

Green   This is one of our family's favorites. It's one of those feel good can't-stop-tasting kinda meals!!

Blue   This sort of tastes like an enchilada, lasagna style. If you love sour cream and salsa with your enchilada, you'll want some with this! A soya hamburger substitute works great as well! Remember, avocados are so good for your body and skin, however, they are very high in fat. If you are monitoring fat for health reasons you may want to have this salad with a meal that's extremely low in fat. Simply serve this with another type of salad. The salad has 6.26 g of fat per serving.

Yellow Wings   This is a family hit and fantastic meat free.

Red   This is one of my personal favorites. If you are a pork chop lover, this will be one of your favorites too! Our test families did mention that if the pork chops are too thin, they may be a little dry!

Yellow   Ground meat needs to reach a temperature of at least 160° F to be completely safe. When you boil meatballs it reaches that temperature very quickly. They are more moist than frying. Also, guess what drains away with all that water? Grease, so they're healthier too! Our test families tell us they will never go back to the old way!!

Week 1

Green: Sweet & Tangy Chicken with Rice and California Vegetables

> Our family rating: 9.5
> Your family rating: _____

Blue: Beef Enchilada Casserole with Tomato-Avocado Salad

> Our family rating: 8
> Your family rating: _____

Yellow Wings: Teriyaki Chicken Toss with Spaghettini Pasta

> Our family rating: 10
> Your family rating: _____

Red: Glazed Pork Chops with Rice and Baby Carrots

> Our family rating: 8
> Your family rating: _____

Yellow: Lean Meatballs in Mushroom Gravy, Mashed Potatoes and Mixed Vegetables

> Our family rating: 8.5
> Your family rating: _____

Sweet & Tangy Chicken with Rice and California Vegetables

Instructions:

Don't change yet! Take out equipment.

1. Preheat oven to 350° F.

   Place chicken in a rectangular oven-safe pan with sides. (If using boneless skinless chicken, unroll. If it's a tight fit they can be squished together.)

   Chop onion (finely).

   Combine in a small bowl in this order; chopped onion, brown sugar, ketchup, salsa and spice. Stir together and pour over chicken.

   Bake in **hot oven**, <u>uncovered</u>. Set timer for 50 minutes.

2. Combine rice and water in a different oven-safe pot. <u>Cover</u> and cook in **hot oven** beside chicken. When the timer rings for chicken, both are ready.

3. Rinse vegetables in colander under cold water. Place in a medium size microwave-safe pot or casserole dish <u>with lid</u>. **Microwave** at high for 5 minutes, <u>then let stand</u>.

   Add spices to vegetables. **Microwave** at high for 2 additional minutes just before serving. Butter if you must.

   Our kids go gaga over this chicken dish, enjoy!!

Ingredients:

Take out ingredients.

8-12 boneless skinless chicken thighs (approx 800 g) <u>*or*</u> *large chicken legs, as shown*

1 small onion

1/2 cup <u>each</u> of <u>brown sugar</u> and <u>ketchup</u>
1/4 cup chunky salsa
1/8 tsp <u>each</u> of <u>cayenne</u> and <u>Mrs. Dash Original Seasoning</u>

1-1/2 cups white rice (Uncle Ben's Brand)
3 cups water

1 pkg (500 g) Green Giant California Style frozen vegetables

1/8 tsp <u>each</u> of <u>rosemary</u> and <u>fresh ground pepper</u>
butter or margarine (optional)

<u>Serves 4-6</u>

Eating Time

Equipment List:

Rectangular lasagna or cake pan
Lge oven-safe pot w/lid
Med microwave-safe pot w/lid
Mixing bowl
Colander
Cutting board
Sharp veggie knife
2 lge mixing spoons
Measuring cups & spoons

Per serving:

Calories	436
Fat	6.4 g
Protein	32.4 g
Carbohydrate	62.2 g

Food Choices:

2	Starch
1/2	Fruits + Veg
0	Milk 1%
2 1/2	Sugars
4	Protein
0	Fat
0	Extras

Prep Time

Sweet & Tangy Chicken

Beef Enchilada Casserole
with Tomato-Avocado Salad

Instructions:

Don't change yet! Take out equipment.

1. Preheat oven to 350° F.

    Brown meat in a large nonstick fry pan or wok, at med-high. Stir until meat is no longer pink.

    Chop onion (finely) while meat is browning and add to meat gradually as you cut.

    Add chilies, soup, salsa and cheeses to cooked meat. Stir until well mixed.

    If you like things spicy, you can add a little chili-garlic sauce to this step.

    Layer in a rectangular lasagna or cake pan in this order; 1/3 dry noodles and 1/3 sauce. Do this **2 more times**.

    Drizzle water all over and top with grated cheese.

    <u>Cover</u> tightly with foil and bake in **hot oven**. Set timer for 50 minutes.

2. Peel avocados. Cut avocados and tomatoes into small pieces.

    Chop onions into small chunks and toss these together in a salad bowl.

    Drizzle with oil, garlic and spices. <u>Cover</u> and **refrigerate** until serving. *You can throw this on a bed of washed lettuce if you want to get fancy schmancy.*

3. *When timer rings for the casserole take it out and let stand for about 5 minutes before serving.

Eating Time

Ingredients:

Take out ingredients.

675 g ground beef (90 % lean)

1 small onion

1 can (127 mL) chopped green chilies (Old El Paso)
1 can (284 mL) Cheddar cheese soup (Campbell's)
1 cup chunky salsa
1/2 cup <u>each</u> of <u>grated low-fat Cheddar cheese</u> and <u>grated part-skim mozzarella cheese</u>

12 Catelli Express Oven-Ready lasagna noodles (approx...it depends on pan size)

2/3 cup water
1/2 cup <u>each</u> of <u>grated low-fat Cheddar</u> and <u>grated part-skim mozzarella cheeses</u>
aluminum foil

2 avocados (400 g)
4 Roma tomatoes

2 green onions

1 Tbsp olive oil
1/2 tsp prepared garlic
1/8 tsp <u>each</u> of <u>salt</u> and <u>lemon pepper</u>

Our family likes to have a little fat-free sour cream and salsa on the side. It's soooo good!!!

<u>Serves 6-8</u>

Equipment List:

Lge non-stick fry pan or wok
Rectangular lasagna or cake pan
Salad bowl
Aluminum foil
Cheese grater
Cutting board
Sharp veggie knife
Can opener
Lge mixing spoon
Measuring cups & spoons

Per serving:

Calories	494
Fat	26.3 g
Protein	29.1 g
Carbohydrate	35.3 g

Food Choices:

1 1/2	Starch
1	Fruits + Veg
0	Milk 1%
0	Sugars
3 1/2	Protein
3 1/2	Fat
0	Extras

Prep Time

Beef Enchilada Casserole

Teriyaki Chicken Toss with Spaghettini Pasta

Instructions:

Don't change yet! Take out equipment.

1. Fill a large **stove-top** pot with water, <u>cover</u> and bring to a boil.

2. Heat oil in large nonstick fry pan or wok at med-high.

   Cut chicken into bite size pieces and gradually add to pan as you cut. Season and stir until meat is no longer pink.

   Chop onion, zucchini and peppers into bite size chunks in that order. Add to pan as you chop.

   Wash and slice mushrooms, adding to pan as you slice. Toss occasionally.

3. Place pasta in boiling water, stir and cook <u>uncovered</u>. Set timer for 8 minutes.

4. Add cornstarch to a small bowl or measuring cup. Gradually add soya while stirring so that the cornstarch is smooth not lumpy. Mix in the honey-garlic sauce and chicken broth. Add to pan of chicken and veggies. Stir and leave to simmer on low.

5. Rinse the **cooked** pasta under hot water in a colander. <u>Let drain</u>. Mix the following in the <u>empty</u> pasta pot at med-low; remaining chicken broth, curry powder, honey and basil. Stir together and return pasta to pot. Toss the pasta to coat in the spiced broth. Remove from heat. Numm!

This would mean yet another awesome supper would be ready to serve now!!

Ingredients:

Take out ingredients.

6 L water (approx)

1 tsp canola or olive oil

3 boneless skinless chicken breasts (approx 450 g)
1/2 tsp Mrs. Dash Original Seasoning
1/2-1 tsp crushed chilies

1 small onion
1 small zucchini
1/2 <u>each</u> of <u>green</u> and <u>red peppers</u>

10 mushrooms

350 g spaghettini pasta (Catelli)

1 Tbsp cornstarch
2 Tbsp soya sauce
1/3 cup V-H honey-garlic sauce
1/4 cup chicken broth (Campbell's)

1 cup chicken broth (remaining broth from 284 mL can)
2 tsp curry powder
1 Tbsp liquid honey
1/2 tsp basil leaves

<u>Serves 4-6</u>

Eating Time

Equipment List:

Lge stove-top pot w/lid
Lge nonstick fry pan or wok
Small mixing bowl
Colander
Cutting board
Sharp meat knife
Sharp veggie knife
Pasta fork
Small & lge mixing spoon
Measuring cups & spoons

Per serving:

Calories	401
Fat	3.4 g
Protein	28.5 g
Carbohydrate	64.0 g

Food Choices:

3	Starch
1/2	Fruits + Veg
0	Milk 1%
1 1/2	Sugars
3	Protein
0	Fat
0	Extras

Prep Time

Teriyaki Chicken Toss

Glazed Pork Chops with Rice and Baby Carrots

Instructions:

Don't change yet! Take out equipment.

1. Preheat oven to broil.
   Place pork chops on a broiler pan. **Broil** just until white in color.

2. Combine rice and water in a large microwave-safe pot with lid. <u>Cover</u> and **microwave** at high for 15 minutes.

3. Rinse carrots in colander under cold water. Combine water, carrots and spice in a medium **stove-top** pot. Set aside.

4. Remove the chops from the oven and flip them cooked side down. <u>Turn oven down to 350° F</u> **on bake**.

   Spread each pork chop thinly with the following **in this order**; prepared mustard, brown sugar, cinnamon and basil.

   <u>Return the chops</u> to **oven** at the lower temperature and bake.

5. When timer rings for rice let it stand for 10 minutes to set. When rice is ready so are chops.

6. Bring vegetables to a boil now, then simmer until rice and pork chops are done and carrots are tender. Drain water and add butter if you must.

Ingredients:

Take out ingredients.

8 pork chops medium thickness boneless and trimmed (approx 700 g)

1-1/2 cups Basmati rice (Uncle Ben's Brand)
3 cups water
For a nice change you can replace half the water with apple juice if you have it on hand. It compliments this dish nicely.

1/4 cup water
1 pkg (500 g) frozen baby carrots (Green Giant)
1/2 tsp Mrs. Dash Original Seasoning

These amounts are **<u>per chop</u>**:
1/2 tsp prepared mustard
1 tsp brown sugar
1/8 tsp <u>each</u> of <u>cinnamon</u> and <u>basil</u>

butter or margarine (optional)

<u>Serves 4-6</u>

30

Eating Time

Equipment List:

Broiler pan
Lge microwave-safe pot w/lid
Med stove-top pot
Colander
Spoon & fork
Lge mixing spoon
Measuring cups & spoons

Per serving:

Calories	388
Fat	8.3 g
Protein	30.2 g
Carbohydrate	48.2 g

Food Choices:

2	Starch
1/2	Fruits + Veg
0	Milk 1%
1 1/2	Sugars
3 1/2	Protein
0	Fat
1	Extras

Prep Time

Glazed Pork Chops

Lean Meatballs in Mushroom Gravy, Mashed Potatoes and Mixed Vegetables

Instructions:

Don't change yet! Take out equipment.

1. Fill a large **stove-top** pot with water. <u>Cover</u> and bring to a boil.

   Mix garlic into meat and shape into <u>tight balls</u>. Gradually add to boiled water as you make them. Set timer for 7 minutes <u>after</u> the last meatball goes into the water.

   Chop onion (finely) and slice mushrooms. When timer rings for meatballs, <u>drain off the water</u> and add mushrooms and onion to the pot. Return to medium heat.

2. Rinse vegetables in colander under cold water. Place in a medium size microwave-safe pot or casserole dish with lid. <u>Cover</u> and **microwave** at high for 5 minutes, then let stand.

3. Boil water in a kettle for the potatoes.

4. Add soup, milk, Worcestershire and spice to meat, onion and mushrooms. Stir until mixture comes to a boil. <u>Cover</u>, reduce heat and simmer for 10 minutes.

5. Prepare potato flakes in a mixing bowl according to package directions, always starting with liquids and ending with flakes. *We use half the required butter.*

6. **Microwave** vegetables at high for an additional 2 minutes, just before serving. Add salt and butter, if you must.
   Tip <u>*Set oven to 375° F before you begin.*</u> *When oven is ready,* <u>*turn it off*</u> *and toss in some fresh unsliced bread, multigrain or focaccia. Any of these are fantastic with this meal.*

Ingredients:

Take out ingredients.

6 L water (approx)

675 g ground beef (90% lean)
1 tsp garlic powder

1 small onion
10 mushrooms

1 pkg (500 g) frozen mixed vegetables (Green Giant)

2-1/2 cups water at least (to allow for boil down)
1 can (284 mL) cream of mushroom soup (Campbell's)
1/2 the soup can 1% milk
1 Tbsp Worcestershire sauce
dash (1/8 tsp) cayenne

1-1/2 cups instant mashed potato flakes (McCain)
*remember to have **1% milk** and **butter** on hand*

1/4 tsp salt (optional)
butter or margarine (optional)
focaccia (optional)

Prep Ahead Option
* If you have the extra time you can peel 4 large potatoes and mash with some 1% milk instead of using instant

<u>Serves 4-6</u>

Eating Time

Equipment List:

Lge stove-top pot w/lid
Med microwave-safe pot w/lid
Kettle
2 mixing bowls
Colander
Cutting board
Sharp veggie knife
Lge mixing spoon
Measuring cups & spoons

Per serving:

Calories	464
Fat	23.9 g
Protein	28.2 g
Carbohydrate	33.9 g

Food Choices:

1	Starch
1 1/2	Fruits + Veg
1/2	Milk 1%
0	Sugars
3 1/2	Protein
3	Fat
0	Extras

Prep Time

Lean Meatballs in Mushroom Gravy

Things You Should Know About the Recipes

Yellow Wings   This is just delicious and definitely a family favorite. Tip: When I only use a part can of broth, I dump the balance in an old margarine container and freeze the rest. I keep a permanent marker in my junk drawer to label the container.

Blue   I recommend you make this dish when you're not running out of the house. It's most successful when you baste the meat regularly keeping the simmer high enough to tenderize, but low enough that the nummy sauce doesn't boil away. I use an electric fry pan.

Red Wings   I hunted for a gigi sauce (Italian tomato cream sauce) that was low in fat and full of flavor. There wasn't one that I could find so I was very proud of myself when I came up with this recipe. It's fantastic even without the chicken. Make sure you have the low-fat Parmesan on hand!!

Yellow Wings   I love the combination of flavors in these fajitas. Our family has no idea they are eating a very healthy meal when we serve this. They think it's junk food! If you saute zucchini instead of meat, this is going to be one of your favorite veggie dishes.

Green   Our test families absolutely love this meat loaf. We do too. All those bad memories of meat sitting in 4 inches of grease can all go away now. This is one of those feel good meals, no grease included! Remember, ketchup for the kids...aaand the big kids! Note: When I make this meal, I double the meat purchase, make two loaves instead of one, plaster both with the sauce and wrap up one for the freezer.

Week 2

2

Yellow Wings: Spicy Shrimp (or Chicken) with Rice and Snow Peas

Our family rating: 10
Your family rating: _____

Blue: Saucy Simmered Chops with Rice and Green Beans

Our family rating: 9.5
Your family rating: _____

Red Wings: Penne Pasta with Italian Gigi Sauce and Vegetables

Our family rating: 10
Your family rating: _____

Yellow Wings: Lean Sirloin Fajitas with Greens and "The Works"

Our family rating: 9.5
Your family rating: _____

Green: Lean No-Loaf Meatloaf with Scalloped Potatoes and Brussel Sprouts

Our family rating: 9.5
Your family rating: _____

Spicy Shrimp (or Chicken) with Rice and Snow Peas

Instructions:

Don't change yet! Take out equipment.

1. Combine rice and water in a large microwave-safe pot or casserole dish with lid. <u>Cover</u> and **microwave** at high. Set timer for 20-25 minutes.

2. Heat oil in a large nonstick fry pan or wok at med-high. Add shrimp, garlic and ginger to pan. Saute 1-2 minutes. (If using chicken instead of shrimp cut into bite size pieces and toss until no longer pink.

   Peel and cut carrot diagonally into thin slices. Add to pan as you cut.

   Rinse snow peas in colander and drain water chestnuts. Add both to pan.

   Combine in this order in a small bowl; ketchup, chicken broth, soya sauce, Worcestershire sauce, brown sugar and cayenne pepper. Blend together and pour over chicken. Stir. <u>Reduce heat and simmer</u> until rice is cooked and left to stand for 5 minutes.

Ingredients:

Take out ingredients.

3 cups water
1-1/2 cups white rice (Uncle Ben's Brand)

1 tsp canola or olive oil
450 g shrimp (can be replaced with 3 chicken breasts)
1 tsp prepared garlic
1/4 tsp ground ginger

1 large carrot

1 pkg (approx 200 g) frozen snowpeas
1 can (284 mL) sliced water chestnuts (drained)

1/2 cup ketchup
1/2 cup chicken broth (Campbell's)
2 Tbsp <u>each</u> of <u>soya sauce</u>, <u>Worcestershire sauce</u> and <u>brown sugar</u>
1/8 tsp cayenne pepper

fresh shrimp for garnish (optional)

<u>**Serves 4-6**</u>

Eating Time

Equipment List:

Lge nonstick fry pan or wok
Lge microwave-safe pot w/lid
Colander
Mixing bowl
Cutting board
Sharp veggie knife
Can opener
Carrot peeler
Lge mixing spoon
Measuring cups & spoons

Per serving:

Calories	343
Fat	3.0 g
Protein	23.9 g
Carbohydrate	55.1 g

Food Choices:

2	Starch
1	Fruits + Veg
0	Milk 1%
1 1/2	Sugars
3	Protein
0	Fat
0	Extras

Prep Time

Spicy Shrimp

Saucy Simmered Chops with Rice and Green Beans

Instructions:

Don't change yet! Take out equipment.

1. Preheat oven to 350° F.

   Spray a large nonstick frying pan with cooking spray. (I use an electric frying pan.)

   Brown chops on both sides at med-high.

   ....while meat is browning....

2. Rinse vegetables in colander under cold water. Place in a medium size microwave-safe pot or casserole dish with lid. <u>Cover</u>, **microwave** at high for 5 minutes, then let stand.

3. Combine rice and water in an <u>oven-safe pot</u> with lid. <u>Cover</u> and place in **hot oven.** Set timer for 55 minutes.

4. Chop celery (finely) and sprinkle over chops.

   Combine brown sugar, ketchup, water, paprika, Worcestershire sauce and drained mushrooms in a bowl. Stir until well mixed and add to pork chop pan. Stir, <u>cover</u> and bring to a boil. <u>Turn down to a simmer</u> until the timer rings for rice. (Check the sauce occasionally.)

5. Add pepper to beans. **Microwave** at high for 2 additional minutes, just before serving. Salt and butter if you must.

Ingredients:

Take out ingredients.

cooking spray (no-cholesterol)

8-12 thin pork chops boneless and trimmed (approx 700 g)

500 g frozen French Style green beans (Green Giant)

3 cups water
1-1/2 cups white or brown rice (Uncle Ben's Brand)

2 stalks of celery

1/2 cup brown sugar
1 cup <u>each</u> of <u>ketchup</u> and <u>water</u>
1 tsp paprika
2 Tbsp Worcestershire sauce
1 can (284 mL) sliced mushrooms (drained)

fresh ground pepper to taste

1/4 tsp salt (optional)
butter or margarine (optional)

<u>Serves 4-6</u>

Eating Time

Equipment List:

Lge nonstick fry pan (or electric)
Lge oven-safe pot w/lid
Med microwave-safe pot w/lid
Mixing bowl
Colander
Cutting board
Sharp veggie knife
Can opener
Lge mixing spoon
Measuring cups & spoons

Per serving:

Calories	494
Fat	8.8 g
Protein	32.9 g
Carbohydrate	71.0 g

Food Choices:

2	Starch
1	Fruits + Veg
0	Milk 1%
3	Sugars
4	Protein
0	Fat
0	Extras

20

Prep Time

Saucy Simmered Chops

Penne Pasta with Italian Gigi Sauce and Vegetables

Instructions:

Don't change yet! Take out equipment.

1. Fill a large **stove-top** pot with water. <u>Cover</u> and bring to a boil.

2. Heat oil in a large nonstick fry pan or wok at med-high.

   Cut chicken into bite size pieces and add to pan as you cut. Add garlic and basil to pan. Toss occasionally until meat is no longer pink.

   ...while meat is browning...
   Sliver onion and add to pan as you chop.

   Wash and slice mushrooms and add to pan as you slice.

3. Rinse vegetables in colander under cold water. Place vegetables and spice in a medium size microwave-safe pot with lid. <u>Cover</u>, **microwave** at high for 5 minutes, then let stand.

4. Place pasta in boiling water, stir and cook <u>uncovered</u>. Set timer for 11 minutes.

5. Combine tomato soup, milk and salsa in a mixing bowl. Pour over chicken mixture.

   Wash and chop green onion. *See page 21 for tip on cutting green onion.* Add to pan and simmer until your timer rings for pasta.

6. Rinse the **cooked** pasta under hot water in a colander. Return to pot. Toss with olive oil and basil.

Ingredients:

Take out ingredients.

6 L water (approx)

1 tsp canola or olive oil

3 boneless skinless chicken breasts (approx 450 g)
2 tsp prepared garlic
1 tsp basil

1/2 small onion

10 mushrooms

1 pkg (500 g) Green Giant Japanese Style frozen vegetables
1/2 tsp Mrs. Dash Original Seasoning

350 g penne pasta (Catelli)

1 can (284 mL) tomato soup (Campbell's)
1/2 the soup can 1% milk
3/4 cup chunky salsa

2 green onions

1 tsp olive oil (optional)
1/2 tsp basil

Optional *After serving the sauce on the pasta my family love to sprinkle low-fat Parmesan and more green onion on top. Nummmm!!*

<u>Serves 4-6</u>

Eating Time

Equipment List:

Lge nonstick fry pan or wok
Lge stove-top pot w/lid
Med microwave-safe pot w/lid
Mixing bowl
Colander
Cutting board
Sharp veggie knife
Sharp meat knife
Can opener
Lge mixing spoon
Measuring cups & spoons

Per serving:

Calories	400
Fat	4.7 g
Protein	28.6 g
Carbohydrate	61.0 g

Food Choices:

3	Starch
1 1/2	Fruits + Veg
0	Milk 1%
0	Sugars
3	Protein
1/2	Fat
0	Extras

Prep Time

Snacks

L. BENNETT

Italian Gigi Sauce on Pasta

Lean Sirloin Fajitas with Greens and "The Works"

Instructions:	Ingredients:

Don't change yet! Take out equipment.

Take out ingredients.

1. Preheat oven to 350° F.

2. Heat oil in a large nonstick fry pan or wok at med-high. Cut meat into thin strips against the grain and add to pan as you cut. Toss occasionally until meat is no longer pink. Add spices to meat while it's browning.

1 tsp canola or olive oil
450 g of lean boneless sirloin steak
This can be replaced with chicken.

1 tsp each of cumin, chili powder, and prepared garlic
fresh ground pepper to taste

Sliver onion and peppers in that order. Add to pan as you cut and stir.

1 small onion (purple if possible)
1 small green pepper
1 small red pepper

3. When oven is ready, turn it off. Wrap the tortillas up in foil and toss into **prewarmed** oven.

8 large soft tortillas (Old El Paso)
aluminum foil

4. Add salsa, Worcestershire sauce and vinegar to meat pan. Stir until well blended.

These are your toppings.

3/4 cup chunky salsa
1 Tbsp each of Worcestershire sauce and red wine vinegar

5. Wash and slice **green onion**.
Chop tomatoes and grate **cheese**.
Break **lettuce** into salad spinner, rinse with cold water, and spin dry.

2 green onions
4 Roma tomatoes
1 cup grated low-fat Cheddar cheese
1 small head lettuce
Use the leftovers for a salad another day.

6. Spoon meat mixture onto centre of warmed tortilla, fold up bottom and then fold over sides.

Load on your favorite toppings. You may enjoy some extra salsa and no-fat sour cream.

fat-free sour cream and extra salsa
(optional)

Serves 4-6

Eating Time

Equipment List:

Lge nonstick fry pan or wok
Salad spinner
Aluminum foil
Cheese grater
Cutting board
Sharp meat knife
Sharp veggie knife
Lge serving spoon
Lge mixing spoon
Measuring cups & spoons

Per serving:

Calories	335
Fat	10.4 g
Protein	25.5 g
Carbohydrate	34.9 g

Food Choices:

1 1/2	Starch
1	Fruits + Veg
0	Milk 1%
0	Sugars
3	Protein
1	Fat
0	Extras

Prep Time

Lean Sirloin Fajitas

Lean No-Loaf Meatloaf with Scalloped Potatoes and Brussel Sprouts

Instructions:

Don't change yet! Take out equipment.

1. Preheat oven to 375° F.

   Mix together beef, corn flake crumbs, ketchup, Worcestershire sauce, egg white and spices in a mixing bowl. Shape into a loaf on a broiler pan.

   ...in the used bowl...
   Mix together ketchup, brown sugar, Worcestershire sauce and cayenne.

   Spread over entire surface of formed beef with a spoon or spatula.

   Bake in **hot oven**. Set timer for 50 minutes.

2. Boil water in a kettle for the potatoes.

3. Rinse vegetables in colander under cold water. Place in a med size microwave-safe pot or casserole dish with lid. Cover, **microwave** at high for 6 minutes, then let stand.

4. Prepare potatoes in an oven-safe casserole dish with lid, according to the package directions. *We use half the required butter.* Place in **oven** next to meat. When timer rings for meat, both are ready.

5. Add spice to vegetables. **Microwave** at high for 2 additional minutes, just before serving. Add butter if you must.

Ingredients:

Take out ingredients.

900 g ground beef (90% lean)
1/2 cup each of corn flake crumbs and ketchup
1 Tbsp Worcestershire sauce
1 egg white
fresh ground pepper to taste
1 tsp garlic powder

1/4 cup each of ketchup and brown sugar
1 Tbsp Worcestershire sauce
1/8 tsp cayenne pepper

2 cups of water (at least, to allow for boil down)

1 pkg (500 g) Green Giant frozen brussel sprouts

1 pkg (166 g) scalloped potatoes (can be replaced with packaged Cheddar potatoes) *remember to have* **1% milk** and **butter** *on hand*

1/2 tsp Mrs. Dash Original Seasoning
1/4 tsp salt (optional)
butter or margarine (optional)

Serves 4-6

55

Eating Time

Equipment List:

Broiler pan
Oven-safe casserole w/lid
Med microwave-safe pot w/lid
Kettle
Mixing bowl
Colander
Spoon or spatula
Measuring cups and spoons

Per serving:

Calories	588
Fat	26.5 g
Protein	37.5 g
Carbohydrate	50.0 g

Food Choices:

1 1/2	Starch
1/2	Fruits + Veg
1/2	Milk 1%
2	Sugars
4 1/2	Protein
3	Fat
0	Extras

Prep Time

Lean No-Loaf Meatloaf

Things You Should Know About the Recipes

Blue

I can't tell you how many times I heard, "I'm not really a zucchini fan." We had so much fun counting the converts. Our test families tell us that this is really delicious and even better the next day!

Yellow

We literally had to force people to try these sausages. People often equate sausage with high fat. Well, when cooked this way you're left with lean spiced meat. 700 grams of sausage turns into about 470 grams of meat. Neat huh!! Sometimes it's all in the way you do it! This ended up being one of the absolute favorites amongst our families.

Red Wings

This soup is to die for! It's excellent as a quick dinner, a light meal or what our family does sometimes is lay out buns with a variety of sandwich fillers for a heartier meal. The kids like this almost as much as surprising them with pizza!

Green

Remember to look at the section, "A different way of doing things=speed." On page 20 there is a great visual illustration on how to cut a roast for one hour cooking. Our test families raved about this roast dinner. You can increase the size for entertaining, because of the way it's cut. Remember to increase the spices too!

Yellow Wings

Oh boy do we love this meal!! The kids like to roll the rice up like a tortilla in the lettuce leaf. We just put the rice on top of the lettuce and eat it with a knife and fork. The peanut sauce is absolutely delicious. Spread sparingly along the satay. Remember not to overcook the chicken or they get dry. Once the chicken has turned white it's time to flip them.

Week 3

Blue: Zucchini Parmesan with Garlic Bread and Salad

> Our family rating: 9.4
> Your family rating: _____

Yellow: Lean Dry-Garlic Beef Sausage with Linguine and Mixed Vegetables

> Our family rating: 8.7
> Your family rating: _____

Red Wings: Mushroom Cheddar Soup with Bread Sticks

> Our family rating: 10
> Your family rating: _____

Green: Quick Roast with New Potatoes and Baby Carrots

> Our family rating: 9
> Your family rating: _____

Yellow Wings: Thai Satay with Rice in Lettuce Leaves

> Our family rating: 10
> Your family rating: _____

Zucchini Parmesan with Garlic Bread and Salad

Instructions:

Don't change yet! Take out equipment.

1. Preheat oven to 375° F.
    Cut zucchini into 3/8" thick slices.

    Spread 4 Tbsp of sauce over the bottom of a rectangular lasagna or cake pan.

    Layer in this order; 1/2 the <u>dry noodles</u>, 1/2 the mushrooms, 1/2 the mushroom liquid, and 1/2 the zucchini. Sprinkle with corn flake crumbs and Parmesan cheese.

    Use 1/2 the jar of sauce **one spoon at a time over each zucchini slice**.

    Sprinkle 1/2 the grated cheese over top.

    Repeat layers one more time, however, on second layer, scatter cottage cheese between the mounds after the corn flake crumbs and then continue.

    Fill the sauce jar 1/4 full of water, shake, then gently pour between all the zucchini mounds. <u>Cover</u> tightly and bake in **hot oven**. Set timer for 50 minutes.

2. Slice bread in half lengthwise and lightly spread butter over both sides. Sprinkle with garlic powder and parsley flakes. Let stand.

3. Tear lettuce into bite size pieces into the salad spinner. Rinse under cold water and spin dry. **Refrigerate** in a bowl until ready.

4. Remove Parmesan when timer rings and let stand to set. <u>Turn oven off</u> and put the garlic bread in the prewarmed oven, butter side up.

5. Chop apple, into small cubes directly into the salad bowl. Add dressing and toss until coated.

Ingredients:

Take out ingredients.

3 medium zucchini (approx 500 g)

1 jar (700 mL) Catelli Garden Select pasta sauce *Spicy Onion and Garlic*
10 Catelli Express lasagna noodles
1 can (284 mL) sliced mushrooms <u>with liquids</u>
3 Tbsp per layer <u>each of corn flake crumbs</u> and <u>grated low-fat Parmesan cheese</u>

2 cups grated part-skim mozzarella cheese (1 cup per layer)

1 cup 1% cottage cheese

1 French loaf
2 Tbsp butter or margarine (approx)
1/2 tsp garlic powder
1/2 tsp parsley flakes

1 large head green leaf lettuce

1 apple (unpeeled)
1 Tbsp strong gourmet Caesar dressing
3 Tbsp lowest-fat mayonnaise
Optional My family love croutons on any salad.

<u>Serves 6-8</u>

Eating Time

Equipment List:

Rectangular lasagna or cake pan
Salad spinner
Salad bowl
Aluminum foil (for lasagna pan)
Cheese grater
Cutting board
Sharp veggie knife
Bread knife
Butter knife
Can opener
Small mixing spoon
Measuring cups & spoons

Per serving:

Calories	505
Fat	14.0 g
Protein	24.5 g
Carbohydrate	70.2 g

Food Choices:

3 1/2	Starch
1 1/2	Fruits + Veg
0	Milk 1%
0	Sugars
2	Protein
2	Fat
0	Extras

20

Prep Time

3

Zucchini Parmesan

Lean Dry-Garlic Beef Sausage with Linguine and Mixed Vegetables

Instructions:

Don't change yet! Take out equipment.

1. Preheat oven to broil.

    Cut sausages in half lengthwise using a sharp meat knife.

    Face sausages open side down on rack of broiler pan. **Broil** in oven approx 10 minutes or until brown.

2. Fill a large **stove-top** pot with water. <u>Cover</u> and bring to a boil.

    ...meanwhile...

3. Rinse vegetables in colander under cold water. Place in a small microwave-safe pot or casserole dish <u>with lid</u>. **Microwave** at high for 5 minutes, then let stand.

4. Remove sausages from oven and drain grease from broiler pan. Remove rack.

    <u>Reset oven to 400° F.</u>

    Place sausages in bottom of broiler pan and pour sauce over top. Bake in **hot oven**. (about 15 minutes until pasta is cooked and drained and vegetables are heated)

5. Place pasta in boiling water, stir and cook <u>uncovered</u>. Set timer for 9 minutes.

6. Add spices to vegetables. <u>Cover</u> and **microwave** at high for 2 additional minutes just before serving. Butter if you must.

7. Rinse the cooked pasta under hot water in a colander. Return to pot.

Ingredients:

Take out ingredients.

700 g thick beef sausage *or if using small as shown do not cut in half - make a slit and cook slit side down*

6 L water (approx)

2 cups Green Giant frozen baby carrots <u>mixed with</u>
2 cups Green Giant frozen cut broccoli

1 jar (341 mL) V-H dry-garlic sauce

375 g linguine pasta (Catelli)
for a nice change use Catelli Healthy Harvest whole wheat pasta

fresh ground pepper to taste
salt (optional)
butter or margarine (optional)

My family loooves this meal. We serve the pasta as a side dish and drizzle a little sauce directly on the pasta. It gives it a nice almond color and tastes great!!.

<u>Serves 4-6</u>

Eating Time

Equipment List:

Broiler pan
Lge stove-top pot w/lid
Small microwave-safe pot w/lid
Colander
Cutting board
Sharp meat knife
Pasta fork
Small mixing spoon
Measuring cups & spoons

Per serving:

Calories	621
Fat	22.2 g
Protein	20.4 g
Carbohydrate	84.8 g

Food Choices:

3	Starch
1/2	Fruits + Veg
0	Milk 1%
3 1/2	Sugars
2	Protein
3 1/2	Fat
0	Extras

Prep Time

3

Dry-Garlic Beef Sausage

Mushroom Cheddar Soup with Bread Sticks

Instructions:

Don't change yet! Take out equipment.

1. Preheat oven to 400° F.

2. Heat oil at med-high in a large **stove-top** pot.

   Chop onion (finely). Wash and slice mushrooms. *See page 20 for a fast way to cut mushrooms.* Add to oil as you cut, beginning with onion. Saute until onion looks transparent.

   Add soup, gradually add milk and stir until smooth.

   Stir in cheese.

   <u>Reduce heat</u> to simmer for 5-7 minutes. Stir.

3. Make a slit along the top of the bread sticks just breaking the surface. Brush with butter. Sprinkle with garlic powder and low-fat Parmesan cheese, then place on cookie sheet with edges.

   Bake in **hot oven** for 5 minutes or until golden brown.

Ingredients:

Take out ingredients.

1 tsp canola oil or olive oil

1 small onion
10 mushrooms

2 cans (284 mL each) cream of mushroom soup (Campbell's)
2 soup cans 1% milk

1/2 cup grated low-fat Cheddar cheese

12 (brown to serve) bakery Italian bread sticks
1 Tbsp melted butter or margarine
1/4 tsp garlic powder
1 Tbsp grated low-fat Parmesan cheese

Option *I often replace the bread sticks with buns and throw sandwich fillers on the table. It's kind of a fun meal!*

<u>**Serves 4-6**</u>

Eating Time

Equipment List:

Cookie sheet w/edges
Lge stove-top pot
Cheese grater
Cutting board
Sharp bread knife
Sharp veggie knife
Pastry brush
Can opener
Lge mixing spoon
Measuring cups & spoons

Per serving:

Calories	349
Fat	13.2 g
Protein	12.9 g
Carbohydrate	44.7 g

Food Choices:

2	Starch
1/2	Fruits + Veg
1	Milk 1%
1/2	Sugars
1/2	Protein
2 1/2	Fat
0	Extras

Prep Time

3

Mushroom Cheddar Soup

Quick Roast with New Potatoes and Baby Carrots

GREEN

●■▲

Instructions:

Don't change yet! Take out equipment.

1. Preheat oven to 385° F.

    Flip roast fat side down and make 1/2 inch slices 3/4 of the way down, from top to bottom, leaving fatty surface intact. *(See page 20 for illustration.)* Turn roast fat side up. Place in large roasting pan and sprinkle roast on all sides with spices.

    Scrub potatoes. (**Chop into medium sized chunks if using large potatoes.**) Chop onions in bite size chunks and slice celery. Arrange around roast along with baby carrots and <u>whole</u> washed mushrooms.

    Pour broth over roast and vegetables and toss in a bay leaf. <u>Cover</u> and bake in **hot oven**. Set timer for 55 minutes.

    Mix flour and Bisto together in a small bowl and gradually add water. Stir until smooth, then set aside.

    Check your roast when timer rings. *It may need a few more minutes depending on how you like it.*
    Transfer roast and vegetables to serving platter.

    Place the roasting pan on **stove-top** at med-high. Add <u>flour mixture</u> to drippings <u>just before serving</u>. Stir until smooth and thickened.

Ingredients:

Take out ingredients.

900 g beef sirloin roast (boneless and trimmed)

1 tsp each of <u>thyme leaves</u>, <u>marjoram leaves</u> and <u>prepared garlic</u> sprinkle of salt
****Remember** If you increase the size of the roast you must increase the amount of spice.

16 small new potatoes (1 kg) or 4 large
1 onion
2 celery stalks
1 pkg (454 g) washed and peeled baby carrots (from the produce dept)
8 whole mushrooms

1 can (284 mL) beef broth (Campbell's)
1 bay leaf

2 Tbsp <u>each</u> of <u>flour</u> and <u>Bisto</u> Brown Gravy Mix
1/3 cup water

My kids are not too crazy about roast, but this version got a (9) family rating. They don't all looove every component, but the combination of flavors make this a hit for the family. It's a great entertaining dish as well!!!
      You'll even get to visit!!!

<u>**Serves 4-6**</u>

Eating Time

Equipment List:

Roasting pan
Serving platter
Small bowl
Cutting board
Sharp meat knife
Sharp veggie knife
Can opener
Lge mixing spoon
Measuring cups & spoons

Per serving:

Calories	431
Fat	6.4 g
Protein	38.5 g
Carbohydrate	54.8 g

Food Choices:

3	Starch
1	Fruits + Veg
0	Milk 1%
0	Sugars
5	Protein
0	Fat
0	Extras

15

Prep Time

3

Quick Roast

Thai Satay with Rice in Lettuce Leaves

Instructions:

Don't change yet! Take out equipment.

1. Combine rice and water in a **stove-top** pot <u>with lid</u>. Bring to a boil then simmer for 20-25 minutes, then let stand

2. Combine soya, brown sugar and cayenne pepper in a mixing bowl.
   Cut chicken into long strips, approx 5 strips per breast.
   Place chicken strips in soya mixture as you cut them. Stir to submerge. Let soak in **fridge**.

3. Rinse <u>whole lettuce leaves</u> under cold water, pat dry and leave in **fridge** until serving.
   Make a mixture of dressing, brown sugar and crushed chilies in a small bowl. <u>Set aside on serving table</u>.

   Set oven to <u>broil</u>.

4. Place peanut butter in a small microwave-safe bowl. Soften in **microwave** 20-25 seconds or until it's slightly runny. Add brown sugar, soya, spices and water. Keep stirring with fork until well blended. Add water until smooth and just a little runny. <u>Set aside on serving table</u>.

5. Skewer chicken on bamboo skewers and place on a cookie sheet (with edges). **Broil** until chicken is no longer pink, flip them over and cook until other side is no longer pink. (<u>Don't overcook!</u>)

6. Serve the chicken on each plate. Serve a leaf of lettuce with a large spoon of rice in the middle. Drizzle a tiny bit of the sundried dressing mixture over the rice.   Fold it up like a taco or leave it flat and eat it with a knife and fork.
   Either way, it's delicious!!

Ingredients:

Take out ingredients.

1-1/2 cups white rice (Uncle Ben's Brand)
3 cups water

1/2 cup soya sauce
1/8 cup brown sugar
1/8 tsp cayenne pepper
4 large boneless skinless chicken breasts (approx 700 g)

1 head green leaf or Romaine lettuce

3/4 cup sundried tomato & oregano salad dressing
1/4 cup brown sugar
1/8 tsp crushed chilies

1-1/2 Tbsp lower-fat creamy peanut butter
1 tsp brown sugar
1 Tbsp soya sauce
1/8 tsp cumin powder
1/8 tsp cayenne pepper
water to smooth (approx 2 tsp)

bamboo skewers

The peanut sauce is to spread sparingly on each piece of chicken after it's cooked. I like to place it in a serving bowl on the table because...some will like it, some won't.

<u>Serves 4-6</u>

Eating Time

Equipment List:

Cookie sheet w/edges
Med stove-top pot w/lid
Mixing bowl
1 small bowl
1 small microwave-safe bowl
Paper towels
Bamboo skewers
Cutting board
Sharp meat knife
Fork
2 small mixing spoons
Measuring cups & spoons

Per serving:

Calories	467
Fat	11.8 g
Protein	35.6 g
Carbohydrate	54.7 g

Food Choices:

2	Starch
0	Fruits + Veg
0	Milk 1%
2 1/2	Sugars
4 1/2	Protein
2	Fat
0	Extras

Prep Time

3

Making Ice Cubes

L. BENNETT

Thai Satay

Things You Should Know About the Recipes

Red Wings

This is such a great spaghetti sauce and it freezes beautifully. Remember the recipe is designed to take half out right away, <u>before you serve</u>, to freeze for when you are making your leftover lasagna. This dish is absolutely perfect with a soya hamburger replacement.

Yellow

If you are making this dish vegetarian style, make everything exactly the same except you won't saute the meat. Once the sauce is thrown together in the baking pan, cut bite size chunks of firm tofu directly into the pan. Then continue with the biscuits. Either way this is an absolutely fantastic pot pie and a huge favorite with the test families.

Blue

You may never make Florentine the long way again! To say this is a family favorite would be a gross understatement! Try entertaining with this dish, especially if you're not the world's greatest cook. People will be amazed!!

Red Wings

If you are a salmon lover, you're going to flip over this recipe. With practice you will be able to get this on the table in about 20 minutes. If I was to pick just one recipe from the book as a favorite, I would have to pick this!! Remember the paper bag needs to be a heavier weight. I save my heavy bakery bags. If you can't find a thick one, just put one lunch bag inside another. If you do this you will need to separate the salmon into two different sacks. In other words you will need 4 thin bags in total. The tartar sauce on the back pocket is a must!

Green

Many of our test families tell us they can now pull this preparation off in about 10 minutes. Remember, ...it's very important to add that extra jar of sauce to the sauce you made for your spaghetti. This is because oven-ready lasagna noodles need liquid to cook properly. The lasagna must also be covered tightly to create steam. If you want the best success, use the specific noodles we recommend.

Week 4

Red Wings: Spaghetti with Lean Spicy Meat Sauce
and Garlic Bread

> Our family rating: 9
> Your family rating: _____

Yellow: Chicken Pot Pie with Green Leaf Salad

> Our family rating: 9.5
> Your family rating: _____

Blue: Quicky Chicken Florentine with
Penne Pasta and Vegetables

> Our family rating: 10
> Your family rating: _____

Red Wings: Salmon Filets with Rice and
Mediterranean Vegetables

> Our family rating: 10
> Your family rating: _____

Green: Lean Leftover Lasagna with Apple-Caesar
Salad and Bread Sticks

> Our family rating: 9.5
> Your family rating: _____

Spaghetti with Lean Spicy Meat Sauce and Garlic Bread

Instructions:

Don't change yet! Take out equipment.

1. Preheat oven to 350° F.

2. Fill a large **stove-top** pot with water. <u>Cover</u> and bring to a boil.

3. Brown meat at med-high in a large nonstick pot until meat is no longer red.

   Chop onion and green pepper (finely). Add to meat as you chop and stir.

   Wash and slice mushrooms. Add to pan as you slice.

   Add sauce to **cooked** meat and stir. Reduce heat and simmer for 15 minutes.

4. Place pasta in boiling water and stir. Cook <u>uncovered</u> for 10 minutes.

5. Slice bread lengthwise, lightly butter and sprinkle with garlic powder and parsley.

   <u>Turn oven off</u> and toss bread in, butter side up.

6. <u>**RESERVE** half the sauce</u>, **before you serve,** <u>for the evening you make lasagna.</u> <u>This freezes beautifully</u>.

I like to rinse my pasta in a colander with hot water, return it to the pasta pot, and toss with a little olive oil and basil.

Ingredients:

Take out ingredients.

6 L water (approx)

450 g ground beef (90% lean)

1 onion
1/2 green pepper or 1 small

10 mushrooms

2 jars (700 mL each) Catelli Garden Select pasta sauce *Spicy Onion & Garlic*

350 g spaghetti pasta (Catelli)

1 baguette or French loaf
2 Tbsp butter or margarine
1/2 tsp garlic powder
1/2 tsp parsley flakes

1 tsp <u>each</u> of <u>olive oil</u> and <u>basil</u> (optional)

<u>Serves 4-6</u>

Eating Time

Equipment List:

Lge nonstick stove-top pot
Lge stove-top pot w/lid
Colander
Cutting board
Sharp veggie knife
Sharp bread knife
Butter knife
Pasta fork
Lge mixing spoon
Measuring spoons

Per serving:

Calories	568
Fat	15.2 g
Protein	21.8 g
Carbohydrate	86.2 g

Food Choices:

5	Starch
1	Fruits + Veg
0	Milk 1%
0	Sugars
1 1/2	Protein
2	Fat
0	Extras

Prep Time

4

Spaghetti with Lean Spicy Meat Sauce

Chicken Pot Pie with Green Leaf Salad

Instructions:

Don't change yet! Take out equipment.

1. Preheat oven to 400° F.

    Heat oil in a large nonstick wok or **stove-top** pot on med-high.
    Cut chicken into bite size pieces and gradually add to pan as you cut. Toss until chicken is no longer pink.

    ...while meat is browning...
    Chop onion (finely). Wash and slice mushrooms, in that order, <u>adding to meat pan</u> as you cut. Add spices and stir.

    Add to pan in this order; butter, flour and gradually add milk. Stir until thickened.

    Rinse vegetables under cold water in a colander. Add vegetables to meat pan, stirring until mixed. <u>Cover</u> and cook for about 3 minutes. Pour this entire mixture into a rectangular oven-safe baking dish or pan.

2. Separate biscuits and place them on top of chicken mixture.
    Bake in **hot oven**. Set timer for 18-20 min or until biscuits are golden brown.

    ...while pot pie is cooking...
3. Tear lettuce into bite size pieces into salad spinner. Rinse under cold water and spin dry. Transfer to a salad bowl and **refrigerate** until chicken pot pie is ready.
    Pour dressing over salad and toss to coat <u>just before serving</u>.

Ingredients:

Take out ingredients.

1 tsp canola or olive oil

3 boneless skinless chicken breasts (approx 450 g)

1 onion
10 mushrooms
1/2 tsp <u>each</u> of <u>salt</u> and <u>ground sage</u>
1/4 tsp <u>each</u> of <u>marjoram</u> and <u>thyme leaves</u>

1-1/2 Tbsp butter or margarine
1-1/2 Tbsp flour
1 cup 1% milk

1 cup frozen mixed vegetables (Green Giant)

1 pkg (340 g) Pillsbury Country Biscuits
If you don't like the consistency of a dumpling on the bottom of the biscuit, bake the biscuits on a separate pan <u>beside</u> the pot pie.

1 head green leaf lettuce

3 Tbsp low-cal dressing
I like balsamic vinaigrette with this meal.
Optional *grated carrot for garnish aaand my kids loooove their croutons*

<u>**Serves 4-6**</u>

Eating Time

Equipment List:

Lge nonstick stove-top pot or wok
Rectangular lasagna or cake pan
Lge cake pan (optional)
Colander
Salad spinner
Salad bowl
Cutting board
Sharp meat knife
Sharp veggie knife
Lge mixing spoon
Measuring cups & spoons

Per serving:

Calories	333
Fat	7.4 g
Protein	24.8 g
Carbohydrate	41.7 g

Food Choices:

2	Starch
1	Fruits + Veg
0	Milk 1%
0	Sugars
2 1/2	Protein
1	Fat
0	Extras

20

Prep Time

4

Chicken Pot Pie

Quicky Chicken Florentine with Penne Pasta and Vegetables

Instructions:

Don't change yet! Take out equipment.

1. Set oven to 375° F.
    Squeeze the moisture from the spinach in a colander using a fork and sprinkle with spice.
    Cut each breast in half.
    Make a slice down the centre of each half, <u>not cutting all the way through</u>.
    Place each piece, **slit side up**, in the palm of your hand. Spoon a tiny bit of spinach on top.
    Flip the piece, **chicken side up**, on a 9"x9" baking dish. Repeat with all the chicken.

    Mix in a bowl, in this order; soup, mayonnaise, garlic powder, celery salt and curry powder. Stir until smooth. Distribute the sauce equally over top of chicken.

    <u>In another bowl</u>, mix bread crumbs, Parmesan, parsley and oil together. Sprinkle over top of chicken and sauce. Bake in **hot oven**. <u>Set timer for 35 minutes</u>.

2. Fill a large **stove-top** pot with cold water for pasta. <u>Cover</u> and let stand.

3. Rinse broccoli under cold water in a colander.
    Place in a medium size microwave-safe pot or casserole with lid. <u>Cover</u> and **microwave** on high for 5 minutes. **When timer rings for chicken <u>leave it in the oven</u> and...**

4. Bring the water to a boil for pasta now. When water has boiled add pasta and set timer for 11 minutes.
    Rinse the **cooked** pasta in a colander under hot water. Return to pot. Toss with a little olive oil if you wish.

5. Stir broccoli. **Microwave** at high for 2 additional minutes <u>just before serving</u>.
    Add salt and butter if you must.

Ingredients:

Take out ingredients.

100 g frozen chopped spinach
1/2 tsp Mrs. Dash Original Seasoning
4 large chicken breasts (approx 700 g)

If some of the spinach falls out or these don't look perfect, don't worry, this meal looks fantastic after it's baked. By the way, it tastes even better.

1 can (284 mL) cream of mushroom soup (Campbell's)
1/2 cup lowest-fat mayonnaise
1/4 tsp garlic powder
1/8 tsp celery salt
1/2 Tbsp curry powder

1/2 cup fine bread crumbs
3-1/2 Tbsp grated low-fat Parmesan cheese
1 tsp dried parsley
1/2 Tbsp canola oil

1 pkg (500 g) frozen cut broccoli (Green Giant)

1 pkg (375 g) Catelli Healthy Harvest penne pasta *whole wheat*
olive oil (optional)

salt (optional)
butter or margarine (optional)

<u>Serves 4-6</u>

Eating Time

Equipment List:

Lge stove-top pot w/lid
Square baking dish
Med microwave-safe pot w/lid
2 mixing bowls
Colander
Cutting board
Sharp meat knife
Fork & spoon
Measuring cups & spoons

Per serving:

Calories	495
Fat	10.3 g
Protein	40.8 g
Carbohydrate	59.8 g

Food Choices:

3	Starch
0	Fruits + Veg
0	Milk 1%
1 1/2	Sugars
5	Protein
1 1/2	Fat
0	Extras

Prep Time

4

— Always Late —

YEAH...DOESN'T IT BUG YA WHEN YOUR PARENTS ARE LATE!

L. BENNETT

Quicky Chicken Florentine

Salmon Filets with Rice and Mediterranean Vegetables

Instructions:

Don't change yet! Take out equipment.

1. Preheat oven to 350° F.

   Spray a nonstick pan with cooking spray.

   Wash salmon under cold water, pat dry with paper towel and season one side. Saute, **spice side down**, over med-high heat approx 1 minute. <u>Season</u>, turn and saute other side.

   ...while salmon is searing...
   Wet the outside of a paper bag thoroughly under cold water. Spray a large piece of aluminum foil, shiny side up, with cooking spray.

   Arrange the salmon fillets on the foil. Turn edges to prevent leaking and pull the foil into the wide side of the wet bag. Curl the end of the bag tightly and place in **hot oven**.

2. Prepare rice in a medium size microwave-safe pot <u>w/lid</u> (according to package directions) in the **microwave**. (about 12 minutes cooking time and 5 minutes to let stand)

   ...in the uncleaned salmon pan...
3. Heat oil over medium heat. Chop all vegetables into small cubes and gradually add to pan as you chop.

   Add spices to vegetables and stir. <u>Reduce heat</u> and simmer <u>uncovered</u>.

   <u>When timer rings for rice, let stand.</u>

   Elegantly set the table, secretly smirk, and enjoy the look of amazement on your family or guest's faces when you serve this. Turn the oven off, cause all is ready!!!

Ingredients:

Take out ingredients.

cooking spray (no-cholesterol)

4 salmon filets (we use Pink)
(skin removed, approx 200 g each)
2 tsp Mrs. Dash Original Seasoning
1 tsp lemon pepper
1/2 tsp rosemary leaves

1 medium size paper bag (grocery type)
cooking spray (no-cholesterol)
aluminum foil

1 pkg (165 g) Uncle Ben's Fast & Fancy *Mushroom* **rice**

1 tsp olive oil
1/2 <u>each</u> of <u>green pepper</u> and <u>red pepper</u>
1 small zucchini
10 mushrooms
1 Roma tomato

1/2 tsp thyme leaves
fresh ground pepper to taste

Prep ahead option
See back pocket for the best tartar sauce.

<u>**Serves 4-6**</u>

Eating Time

Equipment List:

Nonstick fry pan
Med microwave-safe pot w/lid
Aluminum foil
Paper towels
Med size thick paper bag
Cutting board
Sharp veggie knife
Lge mixing spoon
Measuring spoons

Per serving:

Calories	329
Fat	11.3 g
Protein	30.7 g
Carbohydrate	26.2 g

Food Choices:

1	Starch
1/2	Fruits + Veg
0	Milk 1%
1/2	Sugars
4	Protein
1/2	Fat
0	Extras

Prep Time

4

Salmon Filets with Rice

Lean Leftover Lasagna with Apple-Caesar Salad and Bread Sticks

Instructions:

Don't change yet! Take out equipment.

1. Preheat oven to 375° F.

   <u>Combine a new jar</u> of sauce with the <u>reserved sauce</u> from your fantastic spaghetti dinner. Spread a small amount of meat sauce over the bottom of a rectangular lasagna or cake pan.

   Layer in this order; 1/3 dry noodles, 1/3 sauce, 1/3 Parmesan cheese, 1/3 cottage cheese and 1/3 grated cheese. Repeat layers **two** more times.
   Bake in **hot oven**, <u>covered</u> tightly with aluminum foil. Set timer for 40 minutes.

2. Tear lettuce into bite size pieces, place in salad spinner, rinse under cold water and spin dry. Transfer to salad bowl and let stand in **fridge**.

   Stir together mayonnaise and dressing in a small bowl.   Set aside in **fridge**.

   ...when timer rings for lasagna...

3. <u>Uncover</u> lasagna and <u>return to **oven**</u> on lower rack.

4. Separate and unroll bread sticks. Twist each strip and place on a cookie sheet. Sprinkle with fines herbs, garlic powder and white sugar. Place on middle top rack of **oven**. Set timer for 15 minutes. They are ready when they are golden brown. When bread sticks are done, so is the lasagna.

   ...just before serving...

5. Wash apple and slice into bite size chunks. Toss apples and croutons in with lettuce. Pour dressing over salad and toss to coat.

Ingredients:

Take out ingredients.

reserved sauce from spaghetti dinner
1 jar (700 mL) Catelli Garden Select pasta sauce *Mushrooms & Assorted Peppers*

12 Catelli Express Oven-Ready lasagna noodles
1/2 cup grated low-fat Parmesan cheese
2 cups 1% cottage cheese
1-1/2 cups grated part-skim mozzarella cheese
aluminum foil

1 large head Romaine lettuce

3 Tbsp lowest-fat mayonnaise
1 Tbsp strong gourmet Caesar dressing

1 pkg (311 g) Pillsbury bread sticks
fines herbs to taste
1/4 tsp garlic powder
1/4 tsp white sugar

1 red apple unpeeled
1/2 cup croutons

<u>Serves 6-8</u>

Eating Time

Equipment List:

Cookie sheet w/edges
Rectangular lasagna or cake pan
Salad spinner
Salad bowl
Small bowl
Aluminum foil
Cheese grater
Cutting board
Sharp veggie knife
Lge mixing spoon
Measuring cups & spoons

Per serving:

Calories	542
Fat	17.6 g
Protein	31.7 g
Carbohydrate	64.2 g

Food Choices:

2 1/2	Starch
2	Fruits + Veg
0	Milk 1%
1/2	Sugars
3 1/2	Protein
2	Fat
0	Extras

Prep Time

4

Lean Leftover Lasagna

Things You Should Know About the Recipes

Green

This is a very easy pork chop dish that's sure to please. We like it best with the barbeque sauce recipe on the back cover pocket. The lemon is to be removed before eating. It acts as a tenderizer and is a great garnish for a visual presentation.

Red Wings

This is one of my family's favorites and is also rated as one of the top picks with our test families. If you would like to make this a vegetarian dish, simply omit the meat and increase the veggies, NUMMY!!!

Blue

The people who had this recipe in their test week would pass me on the street, moaning and groaning, and would thank me for this meal! It's so versatile. Kids and adults alike enjoy this flavor. If you don't want potatoes, cook rice in a pot beside the chicken. Many people tell me they bring just the mushroom salad to pot luck suppers. It always gets rave reviews!

Red

This is just delicious, one of my favorite meatball recipes. Make sure you don't boil down the sauce because it is to die for on rice.

Yellow

This supper is like going to a bistro. The sauce, mushrooms and cheese combination are fantastic together. Whether you decide to have this meat-free or with the meat, you are going to love it!!

Week 5

Green: ABC Lemon Pork Chops with Roasted Potatoes, Peas and Carrots

Our family rating: 8
Your family rating: _____

Red Wings: Chicken Primavera with Shanghai Noodles

Our family rating: 10
Your family rating: _____

Blue: Crunchy Chicken with Scalloped Potatoes and Mushroom Salad

Our family rating: 10
Your family rating: _____

Red: Tangy Meatballs with Rice and Mixed Vegetables

Our family rating: 8.5
Your family rating: _____

Yellow: Baked Ham & Swiss with Mushroom Sauce on Croissants and Fresh Fruit

Our family rating: 8.5
Your family rating: _____

ABC Lemon Pork Chops with Roasted Potatoes, Peas and Carrots

Instructions:

Don't change yet! Take out equipment.

1. Preheat oven to broil.
   Place chops on a broiler pan and **broil** at close range, 2 minutes on each side.

   ...meanwhile...

2. Rinse vegetables in colander under cold water. Place in a small microwave-safe pot or casserole dish with lid. <u>Cover</u> and **microwave** at high for 5 minutes, then let stand.

3. <u>Remove chops from oven.</u> Turn chops over, top each chop with garlic powder, barbeque sauce and finely sprinkle with brown sugar. Place an onion and lemon slice on each, in that order.

   Broil for 5 minutes. **<u>Reset oven to 350°F.</u>** <u>Cover pan</u> with foil and bake in **hot oven** on middle rack. Set timer for 35 min.

4. Place potatoes in a separate baking dish. Drizzle with oil, sprinkle with spices, then toss to coat. Bake in **hot oven**, <u>uncovered</u>, beside chops.

   When timer rings for chops, both are ready.

5. Add spices to vegetables. <u>Cover</u> and **microwave** at high for 2 additional minutes just before serving. Butter if you must.

The lemon slice is meant to be removed before eating. The juices slowly release into the sauce and make for a wonderful tenderizer.

Ingredients:

Take out ingredients.

4 large pork chops (approx 400 g) boneless and trimmed
My older kids often have two chops each.

2 cups <u>each</u> of <u>frozen Sweetlets peas</u> and <u>frozen baby carrots</u> (Green Giant)

<u>Per chop:</u>
1/8 tsp garlic powder
1 tsp <u>each</u> of <u>bottled barbeque sauce</u> and <u>brown sugar</u> *omit brown sugar if using barbeque sauce on back pocket*
1 thin onion slice
1 lemon slice

1 can (540 mL) whole potatoes (drained)
1/2 tsp Mrs. Dash Original Seasoning
fresh ground pepper to taste
1/2 Tbsp olive oil

1/4 tsp rosemary
1/2 tsp salt (optional)
butter or margarine (optional)

Prep ahead option *See back pocket for a quick barbeque sauce. We like that best!*

<u>Serves 4</u>

45

Eating Time

Equipment List:

Broiler pan
Square baking dish
Microwave-safe pot w/lid
Colander
Aluminum foil
Cutting board
Sharp veggie knife
Can opener
Small mixing spoon
Measuring cups & spoons

Per serving:

Calories	332
Fat	9.0 g
Protein	28.7 g
Carbohydrate	34.2 g

Food Choices:

1	Starch
1	Fruits + Veg
0	Milk 1%
1	Sugars
3 1/2	Protein
1/2	Fat
0	Extras

Prep Time

ABC Lemon Pork Chops

Chicken Primavera with Shanghai Noodles

Instructions:

Don't change yet! Take out equipment.

1. Heat oil in a large nonstick fry pan or wok at med-high.

   Cut chicken into bite size pieces and gradually add to pan as you chop. Stir until meat is no longer pink.

   Combine in this order in a small bowl; cornstarch, gradually stir in broth, add soya sauce, garlic, ginger and brown sugar. Stir until smooth to make a **sauce**. Set aside.

   Cut onion, broccoli, peppers and mushrooms, in that order, into bite size pieces and add to chicken pan as you chop. Toss for 2-3 min.

   Rinse noodles in a colander under warm water, separating them with your fingers. Add noodles and the sauce to pan and stir until hot.

Our family is usually not fond of Shanghai noodles in a restaurant, but will opt out of going anywhere if we are having what they call, "The stuff with the big noodles."

Ingredients:

Take out ingredients.

1 tsp canola or olive oil

3 boneless skinless chicken breasts (approx 450 g)

1 Tbsp cornstarch
1 can (284 mL) chicken broth (Campbell's)
2 Tbsp soya sauce
1 tsp <u>each</u> of <u>prepared garlic</u> and <u>ground ginger</u>
1 Tbsp brown sugar
If you love spicy food, add dried chili flakes to this step.

1 small onion
1 cup broccoli flowerets
1/2 <u>each</u> of <u>red pepper</u> and <u>green pepper</u>
10 mushrooms

1 pkg (454 g) Shanghai noodles
found fresh, often in produce dept

<u>Serves 4-6</u>

Eating Time

Equipment List:

Lge nonstick wok or fry pan
Small bowl
Colander
Cutting board
Sharp veggie knife
Sharp meat knife
Can opener
Small & lge mixing spoons
Measuring cups & spoons

Per serving:

Calories	247
Fat	3.0 g
Protein	25.8 g
Carbohydrate	29.3 g

Food Choices:

1 1/2	Starch
1/2	Fruits + Veg
0	Milk 1%
0	Sugars
3 1/2	Protein
1/2	Fat
0	Extras

Prep Time

5

Chicken Primavera

Crunchy Chicken with Scalloped Potatoes and Mushroom Salad

Instructions:

Don't change yet! Take out equipment.

1. Preheat oven to 375° F.

    Flatten chicken thighs and place on a broiler pan.

    Brush each piece liberally with barbeque sauce. Sprinkle each with pepper and cover with corn flake crumbs. Cook in **hot oven**, uncovered. Set timer for 50 minutes.

2. Boil water in a kettle for potatoes.

    Prepare potatoes in an **oven-safe** casserole dish with lid, according to package directions. *We only use half the required butter.* Always start with liquids and end with dry. Cover and place in **oven** beside chicken. When the timer rings for chicken, both are ready.

3. Combine sour cream, mayonnaise, lemon juice, bacon bits, sugar and spices in a salad bowl. Stir together until smooth.

    Wash and cut mushrooms in half. *See page 20 for a fast way to cut mushrooms.* Add to sauce in bowl and toss until well coated. **Refrigerate** until served.

Ingredients:

Take out ingredients.

8-12 boneless skinless chicken thighs (approx 800 g) *or drumsticks as shown*

1/3 cup bottled barbeque sauce (or see back pocket)
fresh ground pepper
1/2 cup corn flake crumbs

3 cups boiled water (to allow for boil down)
1 pkg (approx 166 g) scalloped or cheese potatoes
*remember to have **1% milk** and **butter** on hand*

3 Tbsp each of fat-free sour cream and lowest-fat mayonnaise
1 Tbsp each of lemon juice and real bacon bits
1/2 tsp each of white sugar and curry powder
dash salt

20 mushrooms

Serves 4-6

55

Eating Time

Equipment List:

Broiler pan
Lge casserole dish w/lid
Kettle
Salad bowl
Cutting board
Sharp veggie knife
Pastry brush
Lge mixing spoon
Measuring cups & spoons

Per serving:

Calories	369
Fat	9.8 g
Protein	33.4 g
Carbohydrate	36.9 g

Food Choices:

1 1/2	Starch
1/2	Fruits + Veg
1/2	Milk 1%
1/2	Sugars
4	Protein
1	Fat
0	Extras

20

Prep Time

5

Crunchy Chicken

Tangy Meatballs with Rice and Mixed Vegetables

Instructions:

Don't change yet! Take out equipment.

1. Bring water to a boil in a large **stove-top** pot at high. *Use a lid when boiling, it speeds up the process.*

2. Combine rice and water in a large microwave-safe pot or casserole with lid. <u>Cover</u> and **microwave** at high. Set timer for 20-25 min.

3. Form tight meatballs and gradually add to boiling water as you form. Toss meat occasionally to ensure all have been submerged.

   Boil for 7 minutes after the last meatball has been added to the water and the water has reached a full boil.

   Combine in a mixing bowl, in this order; ketchup, brown sugar, gradually stir in water and Worcestershire sauce.

   Chop onion (finely). Add to sauce.

   <u>Drain water from the meatballs and add sauce to meatball pot.</u> Bring to a boil, then <u>cover</u> and reduce heat to a **high simmer** for 15 minutes or until timer rings for rice. Stir occasionally to get that nummy sauce all over them!!

4. Combine vegetables and water in a small **stove-top** pot. Bring to a boil, then <u>reduce heat</u> to a low simmer until the rest of the meal is complete.

   Drain water from vegetables. Add basil, salt and butter if you must.

Ingredients:

Take out ingredients.

6 L water (approx)

1-1/2 cups white or brown rice (Uncle Ben's Brand)
3 cups water

675 g ground beef (90% lean)

1 cup ketchup
1/2 cup brown sugar
3/4 cup water
1 Tbsp Worcestershire sauce
1 small onion

Note *When using a microwave for rice, water may spill over depending on the pot you're using. This doesn't affect the rice, you'll just need to wipe it up. Always let the rice stand for about 5 minutes after cooking...about the time it takes to set the table.*

2 cups <u>each</u> of <u>frozen Peaches & Cream corn</u> and <u>frozen Sweetlets peas</u> (Green Giant)
1/4 cup water

1/2 tsp basil
1/4 tsp salt (optional)
butter or margarine (optional)

<u>**Serves 4-6**</u>

Eating Time

Equipment List:

Lge stove-top pot w/lid
Lge microwave-safe pot w/lid
Small stove top pot
Mixing bowl
Cutting board
Sharp veggie knife
Lge mixing spoon
Measuring cups & spoons

Per serving:

Calories	596
Fat	17.8 g
Protein	30.5 g
Carbohydrate	78.5 g

Food Choices:

3	Starch
1/2	Fruits + Veg
0	Milk 1%
3	Sugars
3 1/2	Protein
2	Fat
0	Extras

Prep Time

5

Banana Hunt

L. BENNETT

Tangy Meatballs

Baked Ham & Swiss with Mushroom Sauce on Croissants and Fresh Fruit

Instructions:

Don't change yet! Take out equipment.

1. Preheat oven to 350° F.

    Heat butter in a nonstick **stove-top** pot or pan at med-high.

    Wash and chop mushrooms and onions adding to pan as you cut. *See page 21 for a fast way to cut green onion.* Stir as you add.

    Stir in flour and gradually add milk until mixture **begins** to thicken.

    Add spices, stir and <u>remove from heat</u>.

    Cut croissants in half, lengthwise. Place bottom halves on a cookie sheet.

    Layer <u>each bottom half</u> in this order; 1 slice ham, 1/4 of the mushroom sauce and one slice of cheese.

    Cover with the top of the croissant. Bake in **hot oven**. Set timer for 15 minutes or until cheese has melted.

    ...while this is baking...

2. Wash and cut melon and nectarines into slices.

    Wash grapes and arrange in a very classy kinda way on the serving plates. Place the croissant alongside.

Now you have this mouth watering bistro type supper that will make your family think you've lost it...aaand we all know you have!!

Ingredients:

Take out ingredients.

1 Tbsp butter or margarine

15 mushrooms
4 green onions

1 Tbsp flour
3/4 cup 1% milk

1/2 tsp fresh ground pepper
1/8 tsp nutmeg

4 large croissants

4 (1/4"thick) slices Black Forest ham (approx 160 g)
If you don't like ham, try shrimp or smoked turkey breast. They all work beautifully with this.
4 slices deli low-fat Swiss cheese (approx 85 g)

1/2 small honeydew melon (approx 400 g)
4 nectarines or 12 apricots **(approx 600 g)**
1 small bunch green grapes (approx 350 g)

<u>**Serves 4**</u>

30

Eating Time

Equipment List:

Cookie sheet w/edges
Med size stove-top pan
Cutting board
Sharp bread knife
Sharp veggie knife
Lge mixing spoon
Measuring cups & spoons

Per serving:

Calories	550
Fat	21.9 g
Protein	24.8 g
Carbohydrate	63.4 g

Food Choices:

1 1/2	Starch
3 1/2	Fruits + Veg
0	Milk 1%
1/2	Sugars
2 1/2	Protein
3	Fat
0	Extras

Prep Time

Baked Ham & Swiss

Things You Should Know About the Recipes

Green This is such a delicious supper. It's sooo easy! This is not only a family hit, but is fantastic for entertaining! Also try this on pasta for a change. It's great!

Red Wings This is kind of fun to make mid week and a great one for older kids to prepare. When I make this with soya hamburger-replacement, you can hardly tell the difference!!

Yellow Wings This is another fabulous pork chop recipe. The test families reminded us once again to stress, ...<u>don't over-cook the chops</u> or they turn out dry!!!

Blue The kids go nuts over this supper!! It's also fantastic meat-free, ...just increase the mushrooms and onion a little. While you are preparing this, it looks really watery. It appears that the liquids and the contents don't match. They do, ...so don't panic! Remember it's important to let it stand for 5 minutes or so to let it set. Also, the reason I have scattered the canned asparagus on the top instead of throughout the layers, is so that people who hate canned asparagus can pull them off. This recipe needs those canned asparagus juices though. Use the name brand. The others don't taste right at times.

Red Wings This is a fabulous weekday stew. I still like to make the one that cooks all day, but it's hard to beat this flavor this fast!!

Week 6

Green: Mushroom Beef with Rice and Vegetables

> Our family rating: 8.9
> Your family rating: _____

Red Wings: Lean Mean Taco Salad

> Our family rating: 9.5
> Your family rating: _____

Yellow Wings   Harvest Chops with Spring Vegetable Rice and Glazed Carrots

> Our family rating: 8
> Your family rating: _____

Blue: Cheesy Asparagus-Chicken Lasagna with Fruit Kabobs

> Our family rating: 9
> Your family rating: _____

Red Wings: Lean Gourmet Sirloin Stew with Buns

> Our family rating: 8.5
> Your family rating: _____

6

Mushroom Beef with Rice and Vegetables

Instructions:

Don't change yet! Take out equipment.

1. Preheat oven to 375° F.

    Spray a medium size casserole dish, with lid, with cooking spray.

    Cut meat into thin strips
    Ask your butcher how to cut your meat according to the grain of the meat. It makes a huge difference in how tender your meat will be.

    Add meat to pan and sprinkle with spices.

    Wash and slice mushrooms and green onions, adding to meat pan as you chop.

    Mix in a bowl, in this order; soup, gradually stir in milk and Worcestershire. Stir well and pour over meat mixture.
    Stir together to combine. <u>Cover</u> and bake in **hot oven**. Set timer for 50 minutes.

2. Combine rice and water in a <u>different oven-safe pot</u> or casserole dish with lid. <u>Cover</u> and place in **hot oven** beside beef dish.

3. Rinse veggies in a colander and toss into a nonstick fry pan or wok. Sprinkle with oil, soya, brown sugar and spices. **Let stand.**

4. Stir rice and meat when timer rings. <u>Return to oven</u>, <u>with lids</u>, and **turn oven off**.

5. Stir-fry veggies at med-high for about 5 minutes. When the veggies are ready sooo is supper. Enjoy!!!

Ingredients:

Take out ingredients.

cooking spray (no cholesterol)

675 g sirloin steak (boneless and trimmed)

1 tsp prepared garlic
1/4 tsp <u>each</u> of <u>celery salt</u> and <u>curry powder</u>

8 mushrooms
3 green onions

1 can (284 mL) cream of mushroom soup (Campbell's)
1/2 the soup can 1% milk
1 Tbsp Worcestershire sauce

1-1/2 cups white or brown rice (Uncle Ben's Brand)
3 cups water

1 pkg (500 g) Green Giant Oriental Style frozen vegetables
1 tsp <u>each</u> of <u>olive oil</u>, <u>soya sauce</u> and <u>brown sugar</u>
1/2 tsp Mrs. Dash Original Seasoning

Note When you stir the meat make sure it's saucy. If not, add a little water.

<u>Serves 4-6</u>

Eating Time

Equipment List:

Lge nonstick wok or fry pan
Lge oven-safe pot w/lid
Med casserole dish w/lid
Mixing bowl
Colander
Cutting board
Sharp veggie knife
Sharp meat knife
Can opener
Lge mixing spoon
Measuring cups & spoons

Per serving:

Calories	422
Fat	11.8 g
Protein	31.8 g
Carbohydrate	47.2 g

Food Choices:

2 1/2	Starch
1/2	Fruit + Veg
0	Milk
1/2	Sugars
3 1/2	Protein
1	Fat
0	Extras

Prep Time

6

Young Chefs

Mushroom Beef

93

Lean Mean Taco Salad

Instructions:

Don't change yet! Take out equipment.

1. Brown meat in a large nonstick fry pan at med-high until meat is no longer red.

    Add chili powder, garlic, beans, and salsa, in that order, to fully cooked meat. Stir, reduce heat and simmer 5 minutes.

2. Chop lettuce, rinse in salad spinner and spin dry.

    Place 1 cup of lettuce on each dinner plate.

    Slice tomatoes, green onions and avocado and arrange on plates. Grate cheese.

3. Distribute meat mixture over centre of salad and sprinkle with cheese.

    Serve with tortilla chips and side dishes of salsa and sour cream.

I like to add a little water to the meat and cover while browning. It not only speeds up the cooking process, it has a health benefit as well. Fat rises to the top. Guess what drains away when you drain the water off?

Ingredients:

Take out ingredients.

450 g ground beef (90% extra lean)

1 Tbsp chili powder
1 tsp prepared garlic
1 can (398 mL) red kidney beans
(drained) *or brown beans if you really hate kidney beans*
1 cup chunky salsa

1 head Romaine lettuce

3 Roma tomatoes
3 green onions
1 avocado (optional)
1 cup grated low-fat Cheddar cheese

1/3 bag tortilla chips (approx 133 g)
(Old El Paso)
1 cup chunky salsa
1 cup fat-free sour cream

20 black olives (optional)

<u>**Serves 4-6**</u>

25

Eating Time

Equipment List:

Lge nonstick fry pan
Salad spinner
Serving bowls
Cheese grater
Cutting board
Sharp veggie knife
Can opener
Lge mixing spoon
Measuring cups & spoons

Per serving:

Calories	428
Fat	20.6 g
Protein	28.1 g
Carbohydrate	32.7 g

Food Choices:

1 1/2	Starch
1/2	Fruits + Veg
1/2	Milk 1%
0	Sugars
3	Protein
2 1/2	Fat
0	Extras

Prep Time

Lean Mean Taco Salad

Harvest Chops with Spring Vegetable Rice and Glazed Carrots

Instructions:

Don't change yet! Take out equipment.

1. Preheat oven to 150º F.

   Spray a large nonstick frying pan with cooking spray and place on **stove-top** at med-high. Season chops on one side, place in pan seasoned side down and then season other side directly in pan.

2. Rinse vegetables in colander under cold water. Place in a small microwave-safe pot or casserole dish with lid. <u>Cover</u> and **microwave** at high for 5 minutes, then let stand.

3. Turn chops over to brown other side. Sliver onion and apple (thinly), in that order, and add to meat pan as you cut.

4. Make rice according to package directions in a **stove-top** pot <u>with lid</u>. (about 20 minutes cooking time and 5 minutes to stand)

5. Remove chops from pan and wrap in foil. Toss into **prewarmed** oven. Remove pan from heat. Stir together flour, curry powder and bouillon granules <u>in chops fry pan</u>. Return to heat.

   Gradually add milk. Stir until **sauce** is smooth and has thickened. Simmer for about 5 minutes.

6. Add mustard, sugar, honey and cinnamon to the carrots. Stir and heat for an additional 2 minutes at high, <u>just before serving</u>. Place chops on serving plate with **sauce** equally distributed over each.

Ingredients:

Take out the ingredients.

cooking spray (no-cholesterol)

4 large 1/2" thick pork chops boneless and trimmed (approx 400 g)
My grown children like 2 each.
fresh ground pepper to taste
1/2 tsp basil

1 pkg (500 g) frozen baby carrots (Green Giant) *Set aside a little more than 1 cup for stew this week.*

1 small onion
1 Red Delicious apple

1 pkg (170 g) Uncle Ben's Classics *Oriental Spring Vegetable* **rice**

<u>**Double sauce if increasing chops.**</u>
2 tsp flour
1/2 tsp <u>each</u> of <u>curry powder</u> and <u>low-sodium vegetable bouillon granules</u>
1/3 cup 1% milk

1 tsp prepared mustard
1/2 Tbsp <u>each</u> of <u>brown sugar</u> and <u>liquid honey</u>
dash cinnamon

<u>**Serves 4**</u>

Eating Time

Equipment List:

Lge nonstick fry pan (or electric)
Med stove-top pot w/lid
Small microwave-safe pot w/lid
Aluminum foil
Colander
Cutting board
Sharp veggie knife
Small & lge mixing spoons
Measuring cups & spoons

Per serving:

Calories	404
Fat	8.3 g
Protein	28.2 g
Carbohydrate	54.0 g

Food Choices:

2	Starch
1 1/2	Fruits + Veg
0	Milk 1%
1	Sugars
3	Protein
1/2	Fat
1	Extras

Prep Time

Harvest Chops

Cheesy Asparagus-Chicken Lasagna with Fruit Kabobs

Instructions:

Don't change yet! Take out equipment.

1. Preheat oven to 350° F.

    Heat oil in a large nonstick fry pan or wok at med-high.

    Cut chicken into bite size pieces and gradually add to oil as you cut. Toss until meat is no longer pink. Add garlic and pepper.

    Sliver onion and slice mushrooms, in that order, and add to chicken as you cut. **Remove from heat** once fully cooked.

    Mix in a small bowl in this order; soup, gradually stir in milk and spices. Stir until smooth.

    Spread a few Tbsp of cheesy liquid over bottom of a rectangular oven-safe cake or lasagna pan, then...

    Layer in this order, 1/3 dry noodles, 1/3, chicken mixture, 1/3 sauce, 1/3 Parmesan cheese and 1/3 mozzarella.

    Repeat layers <u>two more times</u>, however, on the third layer place asparagus on top, drizzle the asparagus liquid evenly all over, then continue with the final layer of cheese.
    <u>Cover</u> tightly with foil, shiny side down, and bake in **hot oven**. Set timer for 50 minutes.

2. Cut fruit into bite size pieces and skewer onto kabobs.

3. <u>Remove lasagna</u> from the oven when timer rings and <u>let it set</u> for <u>5 minutes</u> before serving.

Ingredients:

Take out the ingredients.

1 tsp canola or olive oil

3 boneless skinless chicken breasts (approx 450 g)
1 tsp prepared garlic
fresh ground pepper to taste

1 onion
15 mushrooms

1 can (284 mL) Cheddar cheese soup (Campbell's)
1 soup can filled with 1% milk
1 tsp Mrs. Dash Italian Seasoning

12 Catelli Express Oven Ready lasagna noodles
1/2 cup grated low-fat Parmesan cheese
1-1/2 cups grated part-skim mozzarella cheese

1 can (341 mL) asparagus (save liquids)

aluminum foil

2 nectarines (150 g each)
1 small honeydew melon (800 g)
8 strawberries
skewers

Note When you are making this dish it appears watery, like you screwed up. It eventually thickens up and it's fantastic!!!!

<u>Serves 6-8</u>

Eating Time

Equipment List:

Lge nonstick fry pan or wok
Rectangular lasagna or cake pan
Small bowl
Aluminum foil
Bamboo skewers
Cheese grater
Cutting board
Sharp veggie knife
Sharp meat knife
Can opener
Lge & small mixing spoons
Measuring cups and spoons

Per serving:

Calories	373
Fat	10.2 g
Protein	29.7 g
Carbohydrate	40.7 g

Food Choices:

1 1/2	Starch
1 1/2	Fruits + Veg
0	Milk 1%
1/2	Sugars
3 1/2	Protein
1	Fat
0	Extras

Prep Time

Cheesy Asparagus-Chicken Lasagna

Lean Gourmet Sirloin Stew with Buns

Instructions:

Don't change yet! Take out equipment.

1. Preheat oven to 350° F.

2. Heat oil in a large **stove-top** pot at med-high.

   Cut beef into bite size pieces and gradually add to pot as you chop. Toss until meat is no longer red.

   Add prepared garlic and pepper to meat while it's browning.

   Sliver onion, chop celery and slice mushrooms in half in that order. Add to meat pot as you cut.

3. Turn oven <u>off</u> and place buns in **prewarmed oven**.

4. Rinse carrots in a colander under cold water and add to pot.

   Add the following to pot in this order; canned tomatoes, brown beans, ketchup and whole potatoes (drained). Stir and heat on medium for 10 minutes or until carrots are tender.

   *Yes... really.... that's it... just eat!!! No kidding! Oh!! and **don't forget the buns are in the oven**.*

Ingredients:

Take out the ingredients.

1 tsp canola or olive oil

450 g sirloin steak (boneless and trimmed)

1-1/2 tsp prepared garlic
fresh ground pepper to taste

1 onion
2 celery stalks
10 mushrooms

6 fresh dinner buns

1 cup frozen baby carrots (Green Giant)

1 can (398 mL) chili stewed tomatoes
1 can (398 mL) deep brown beans in sweet sauce
1/2 cup ketchup
2 cans (398 mL each) whole potatoes
(drained)

*Sometimes canned potatoes can be quite large. If they are I slice mine in half.

Serves 4-6

Eating Time

Equipment List:

Lge stove-top pot
Colander
Cutting board
Sharp meat knife
Sharp veggie knife
Can opener
Lge mixing spoon
Measuring cups & spoons

Per serving:

Calories	396
Fat	6.8 g
Protein	25.9 g
Carbohydrate	57.8 g

Food Choices:

2 1/2	Starch
1	Fruits + Veg
0	Milk 1%
1	Sugars
3	Protein
1/2	Fat
0	Extras

Prep Time

Lean Gourmet Sirloin Stew

Things You Should Know About the Recipes

Red Wings   If our family doesn't have curried chicken at least once a month they rebel. This is a fantastic pasta sauce and delicious with or without the chicken.

Green   Our test families go gaga over this shepherd's pie! Soya hamburger replacement works great if you like it the veggie way! *I always add water to the meat pan and put a cover on it. This speeds up the browning and gives me confidence that the ground meat has reached a safe cooking temperature. I also like that the oil exits when draining off the water!

Yellow Wings   This is a great way to have shish-ka-bob with out the skewers. The flavor is amazing. Our test families absolutely love this recipe. If you're a vegetarian try this with chunks of zucchini instead of steak.

Blue   My family feels very special when they are served this meal. It's so easy to prepare and the results are definitely gourmet. Sooo take out the candles, set out the nice dishes and let them all know ...you have lost it!!! Something to think about... Here is the approximate difference in fat when you buy mayonnaise; lowest 0.8 of a gram, low 5.1 grams, and regular 8 to 11 grams. That's per tablespoon folks. Here's what I suggest to those die-hard mayo lovers who looove to spread the high-fat way. Buy both! One for spreading and one for recipes! My test families felt great about this!!!

Yellow Wings   This is like one of those boxed hamburger put together things. This version is just as fast and very healthy. It works out great with the soya hamburger replacement if you happen to fancy it vegetarian style.

Week 7

Red Wings: Curried Chicken with Linguine and Broccoli

Our Family Rating: 10
Your Family Rating: _____

Green: Lean Shepherd's Pie with Multigrain Buns

Our Family Rating: 10
Your Family Rating: _____

Yellow Wings: Teriyaki Unkabobs with Rice

Our Family Rating: 10
Your Family Rating: _____

Blue: Lavish Stuffed Chicken with Roasted Potatoes and Vegetables

Our Family Rating: 10
Your Family Rating: _____

Yellow Wings: Lean Hamburger Jumble with Buns

Our Family Rating: 9.5
Your Family Rating: _____

Curried Chicken with Linguine and Broccoli

Instructions:

Don't change yet! Take out equipment.

1. Heat oil in a large nonstick fry pan or wok at med-high.
Cut chicken into bite size pieces and gradually add to pan as you cut. Toss until meat is no longer pink. Add spices to pan while meat is browning. Stir.

   Chop onion adding to chicken as you cut. Wash and slice mushrooms adding to pan as you cut.

2. Fill a large **stove-top** pot with water. <u>Cover</u> and bring to a boil.

3. Rinse broccoli under cold water in a colander. Place in a medium size microwave-safe pot or casserole with lid. <u>Cover</u> and **microwave** on high for 5 minutes.

4. Add soup to chicken mixture and gradually stir in milk. Continue to stir until well blended.
Simmer at medium heat, stirring often until pasta is ready.

5. Place pasta in boiling water. Stir and cook <u>uncovered</u>. Set timer for 9 minutes.
Rinse the **cooked** pasta in a colander under hot water. Return to pot. Toss with basil and a little olive oil.

6. Stir broccoli and add spice. **Microwave** at high for 2 additional minutes <u>just before serving</u>. Stir in butter if you must!

Ingredients:

Take out ingredients.

1 tsp canola or olive oil

3 boneless skinless chicken breasts (approx 450 g)
2 tsp <u>each</u> of <u>prepared garlic</u> and <u>dried basil</u>
4 tsp curry powder
1/8 tsp cayenne pepper

1 small onion
12 mushrooms
Option *If you are a green pepper nut you can add some to this step as shown.*

6 L water (approx)

1 pkg (500 g) frozen cut broccoli (Green Giant)

1 can (284 mL) cream of mushroom soup (Campbell's)
1/2 the soup can 1% milk

350 g linguine pasta (Catelli)

1 tsp basil
olive oil (optional)

Mrs. Dash Original Seasoning to taste
butter or margarine (optional)

Option *My family looove to sprinkle low-fat grated Parmesan on top.*

<u>**Serves 4-6**</u>

Eating Time

104

Equipment List:

Lge nonstick fry pan or wok
Lge stove-top pot w/lid
Med microwave-safe pot w/lid
Colander
Cutting board
Sharp meat knife
Sharp veggie knife
Can opener
Pasta fork
Small & lge mixing spoons

Per serving:

Calories	397
Fat	7.2 g
Protein	29.4 g
Carbohydrate	53.5 g

Food Choices:

3	Starch
1/2	Fruits + Veg
0	Milk 1%
1/2	Sugars
3	Protein
1	Fat
0	Extras

Prep Time

Curried Chicken

7

● ■ ▲

Lean Shepherd's Pie with Multigrain Buns

Instructions:

Don't change yet! Take out equipment.

1. Preheat oven to 375° F.

   Brown meat in a large nonstick fry pan or wok, at med-high, until meat is no longer red.

   Add ketchup, Worcestershire sauce and spice to **cooked meat**. Stir well.

   Boil water in a kettle (to use later for the instant mashed potatoes).

   Pour meat mixture into a large oven-safe pan or casserole dish.

   Rinse frozen corn in a colander and spread it evenly over the meat mixture.

   Spread the creamed corn over the frozen corn.

   Prepare mashed potatoes according to package directions....<u>always beginning with liquids and ending with flakes.</u> *We use half the required butter.* Top casserole with mashed potatoes. ***If you've never used instant potatoes before they don't look smooth at first. Keep stirring and they look just perfect.***

   Bake in **oven** <u>uncovered</u> for 40 minutes. When the timer rings, **broil** for a few minutes, just to crunch up the top.

2. Take the shepherd's pie out, <u>turn the oven off</u> and <u>toss the buns in</u>. Let the shepherd's pie stand for about 5 minutes while setting the table. *Aaaand don't forget to take the buns out of the oven!*

Ingredients:

Take out ingredients.

900 g ground beef (90% lean)

2/3 cup ketchup
2-1/2 tsp Worcestershire sauce
1-1/2 tsp Mrs. Dash Original Seasoning

3 cups boiling water (to allow for boil down)

1 cup frozen Peaches & Cream corn (Green Giant)

1 can (398 mL) cream style corn (Green Giant)

2 cups instant mashed potato flakes (McCain)
*remember to have **1% milk** and **butter** on hand*

Make ahead choice *If you have time, peel and thinly slice 4 potatoes, bring to a boil and when soft, mash with 1% milk.* ***Do this before you begin instructions.***
Remember to add this to your grocery list.

8 multigrain buns

<u>**Serves 6-8**</u>

Eating Time

Equipment List:

Lge nonstick fry pan or wok
Lge oven-safe pan or
   casserole dish
Kettle
Colander
Mixing bowl
Can opener
Small & lge mixing spoons
Measuring cups & spoons

Per serving:

Calories	512
Fat	20.2 g
Protein	29.9 g
Carbohydrate	52.7 g

Food Choices:

3	Starch
0	Fruits + Veg
0	Milk 1%
1/2	Sugars
3	Protein
2	Fat
0	Extras

Prep Time

Lean Shepherd's Pie

Teriyaki Unkabobs with Rice

Instructions:

Don't change yet! Take out equipment.

1. Combine rice and water in a microwave-safe pot with lid.

   <u>Cover</u> and **microwave** at med-high for 15 minutes.

2. Heat oil in a large nonstick fry pan or wok at med-high.

   Cut meat into large bite size cubes and gradually add to pan as you cut.

   Chop onion and pepper into chunks, in that order, and add to beef as you cut. Wash, then cut mushrooms <u>in half</u> and add to pan.

   Add teriyaki sauce and chili peppers. Stir until hot. <u>Reduce heat</u> and simmer. When timer rings for rice stir and let stand <u>covered</u> for 10 minutes.

   Stir sugar into meat mixture <u>just before serving</u>.

3. Transfer the meat to a <u>covered</u> serving dish and thicken the excess liquids in the uncleaned pan with 1/2 Tbsp of Bisto. Heat until thickened.

   This makes a beautiful sauce for the meat and rice.

Ingredients:

Take out ingredients.

1-1/2 cups Basmati rice (Uncle Ben's Brand)
3 cups water

1 tsp canola or olive oil

900 g sirloin beef steak (boneless and trimmed)

1 onion
1 small green pepper
10 mushrooms

2/3 cup bottled teriyaki sauce
1/2 tsp crushed chili peppers *You can add more if you like things spicy.*

1-1/2 Tbsp brown sugar

1/2 Tbsp Bisto Brown Gravy Mix

<u>Serves 4-6</u>

Eating Time

Equipment List:

Lge nonstick fry pan or wok
Lge microwave-safe pot w/lid
Serving dish w/lid
Cutting board
Sharp meat knife
Sharp veggie knife
Lge mixing spoon
Measuring cups & spoons

Per serving:

Calories	429
Fat	9.0 g
Protein	38.7 g
Carbohydrate	48.4 g

Food Choices:

2	Starch
1/2	Fruits + Veg
0	Milk 1%
1 1/2	Sugars
5	Protein
1/2	Fat
0	Extras

Prep Time

Teriyaki Unkabobs

Lavish Stuffed Chicken with Roasted Potatoes and Vegetables

Instructions:

Don't change yet! Take out equipment.

1. Preheat oven to 375° F.

    Chop broccoli, mushrooms and green onion (finely). Combine with spice in a bowl and stir. Set aside.

    Spray a baking dish or pan with cooking spray. Mound eight equal parts of the broccoli mixture on the baking pan.
    Slice each breast in half and place one piece on the top of each mound of the broccoli mixture. (Don't worry if it looks like it's not going to work, it does!!!)

    ...in the used bowl...
    Combine soup, mayonnaise, garlic powder and celery salt. Spoon evenly over chicken mounds.

    Combine bread crumbs, oil, Swiss cheese and parsley **in a clean bowl**.
    Sprinkle bread crumb mix over the sauce and chicken. Place in **hot oven** <u>uncovered</u>. Set timer for 50 minutes.

2. Scrub potatoes and cut into large cubes. Place <u>in a different oven-safe pan</u> drizzling a small amount of oil over the top. Sprinkle to cover with spices. Toss to coat and place in **hot oven** <u>uncovered</u> beside chicken. When timer rings for chicken, both are done.

3. Rinse vegetables in a colander under cold water. Place in microwave-safe pot <u>with lid</u>. Cook at high for 5 minutes, then let stand.

    Add spices to vegetables. **Microwave** at high for 2 additional minutes <u>just before serving</u>. Butter if you must.

Ingredients:

Take out ingredients.

1 small broccoli floweret
5 mushrooms
2 green onions
1 tsp Mrs. Dash Original Seasoning

cooking spray (no-cholesterol)

4 large boneless skinless chicken breasts (approx 700 g)

1 can (284 mL) cream of mushroom soup (Campbell's)
1/2 cup lowest-fat mayonnaise
1 tsp garlic powder
1/4 tsp celery salt

1 cup bread crumbs
1 Tbsp canola oil
1/2 cup grated low-fat Swiss cheese
2 tsp parsley flakes

4 large potatoes (unpeeled)
1 Tbsp olive oil
1/2 tsp Mrs. Dash Original Seasoning

1 pkg (500 g) Green Giant Oriental Style frozen vegetables

1/4 tsp <u>each</u> of <u>rosemary</u> and <u>fresh ground pepper</u>
butter or margarine (optional)

<u>Serves 4-6</u>

Eating Time

110

Equipment List:

Square baking pan
Oven-safe cake pan
Microwave-safe pot w/lid
2 mixing bowls
Colander
Cutting board
Sharp meat knife
Sharp veggie knife
Can opener
Small mixing spoon
Measuring cups & spoons

Per serving:

Calories	569
Fat	14.3 g
Protein	39.1 g
Carbohydrate	71.0 g

Food Choices:

4	Starch
1/2	Fruits + Veg
0	Milk 1%
1/2	Sugars
4 1/2	Protein
2	Fat
0	Extras

Prep Time

Gourmet Dress-Up

L. BENNETT

Lavish Stuffed Chicken

Lean Hamburger Jumble with Buns

Instructions:

Don't change yet! Take out equipment.

1. Preheat oven to 350° F.

2. Brown meat in a large **stove-top** pot at med-high, until meat is no longer red. Add spices while meat is browning.

    Chop onion and green pepper in small chunks, adding to meat pan as you chop.

    Wash and slice mushrooms, adding to meat pan as you slice.

    Add to pan in this order; salsa, water, pasta sauce, ketchup, Worcestershire sauce, uncooked rotini and corn. Stir until hot and bubbly. Cover and **reduce heat**. Simmer for 15 minutes.

3. Turn oven off and put buns in prewarmed oven.

4. Add cheese to pot just before serving and stir until cheese is melted.

Don't forget the buns are in the oven!

Ingredients:

Take out ingredients.

675 g ground beef (90% lean)
1 Tbsp oregano
1 tsp prepared garlic
1 tsp cumin powder

1 onion
1 small green pepper

10 mushrooms

1 cup chunky salsa
2 cups water
1 can (398 mL) Catelli pasta sauce
Mushroom
1/2 cup ketchup
1 Tbsp Worcestershire sauce
250 g rotini pasta (Catelli)
1 cup frozen Peaches & Cream corn
(Green Giant)

8 dinner rolls

1/2 cup grated low-fat Cheddar cheese

Serves 6-8

Eating Time

Equipment List:

Lge stove top pot w/lid
Cutting board
Sharp veggie knife
Cheese grater
Can opener
Lge mixing spoon
Measuring cups & spoons

Per serving:

Calories	482
Fat	15.7 g
Protein	26.9 g
Carbohydrate	58.2 g

Food Choices:

3	Starch
1	Fruits + Veg
0	Milk 1%
1/2	Sugars
3	Protein
2	Fat
0	Extras

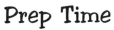

Prep Time

Lean Hamburger Jumble

Things You Should Know About the Recipes

Blue

This has such a fantastic flavor that my mouth is doing little fits right now just thinking about it. If you happen to be a rosemary nut (the spice that is) sprinkle a little more on top of the chicken as well!!!

Yellow

NUUUUM!!! Oh yes...we all like these! When you can make these this fast with this kind of nutritional analysis why buy them ready made? Here's a suggestion. If you have older children who like taking this type of thing for lunch...freak them out a little and involve them in making a triple batch while you are making supper. Wrap them up in wax or plastic wrap and freeze them. Teens say things like, "Yeeea, I made these and froze um." You know, like they do this kind of thing all the time!!

Red Wings

It's tough to beat the flavor of this stir-fry. If you like your food spicier just put the crushed chilies on the table! Remember you can make it meat free. Just throw in a little firm tofu instead of the beef!! If you have older kids, you may want to double the recipe. Our family can't get enough!

Green

Ooooh! I'm licking my lips! This is one of my favorite veggie dishes! Sometimes for a change I replace the cottage cheese with feta. If you do this you must purchase the feta packed in water and drizzle the water all over the prepared lasagna just before adding the last layer of cheese! It's reeeally good! You can only leave the house for 30 minutes, 'cause you need to put the bread sticks in!

Yellow Wings

Ron and I would go to this little Italian restaurant just to get this dish. We would have to share a plate because they used cream and our hearts were chugging as we left. We decided we were going to crack the code for a low-fat version. Here it is!! Our test families raved about this pasta dish. Definitely for entertaining! The cream sauce is great without the chicken.

Week 8

Blue: Roast Chicken with Potato
Wedges and Corn

Our family rating: 8.5
Your family rating: _____

Yellow: Chicken Burritos with Salad

Our family rating: 9.5
Your family rating: _____

Red Wings: Chinese Beef Stir-Fry with Rice

Our family rating: 9.5
Your family rating: _____

Green: Spinach Lasagna with Bread Rolls

Our family rating: 8
Your family rating: _____

Yellow Wings: Hazelnut Chicken with Pasta
and Salad

Our family rating: 10
Your family rating: _____

8

Roast Chicken with Potato Wedges and Corn

Instructions:

Don't change yet! Take out equipment.

1. Preheat oven to 350° F.

    Rinse chicken under cold water tap, inside and out.

    Rub outside of chicken with salt and the inside with basil and rosemary. (This may seem like a disgusting thing to do, but, do it anyway, it's fabulous!!)

    Mix together, in a small bowl, in this order; oil, flour, paprika and then gradually whisk in sour cream.

    Place chicken in a roasting pan or broiler pan and brush with sour cream mixture. Bake in **hot oven** <u>uncovered</u>. Set timer for 55 minutes.

2. Scrub, but don't peel, potatoes and cut into wedges. Toss with oil and spices in a <u>different oven-safe baking dish</u> and **bake** <u>uncovered</u> beside chicken. When timer rings for chicken, potatoes are ready as well.

3. Rinse corn in colander under cold water. Place in a microwave-safe pot or casserole dish <u>with lid</u>. Add pepper and **microwave** at high 5 minutes, then let stand.

    Microwave corn 2 additional minutes at med-high, <u>just before serving</u>. Add salt and butter if you must.

Ingredients:

Take out ingredients.

1.2 kg frying chicken

1 tsp salt
1/2 tsp <u>each</u> of <u>basil</u> and <u>rosemary</u>

1 Tbsp canola or olive oil
1 Tbsp <u>each</u> of <u>flour</u> and <u>paprika</u>
4 Tbsp fat-free sour cream

4 large potatoes
1 Tbsp olive oil
1 tsp prepared garlic
1 tsp dried mint

2 cups frozen Peaches & Cream corn (Green Giant)
fresh ground pepper

salt (optional)
butter or margarine (optional)

<u>**Serves 4-6**</u>

Eating Time

Equipment List:

Roasting pan
Microwave-safe pot w/lid
Small bowl
Colander
Cutting board
Sharp veggie knife
Pastry brush
Small mixing spoon
Measuring cups & spoons

Per serving:

Calories	559
Fat	25.6 g
Protein	27.9 g
Carbohydrate	54.2 g

Food Choices:

3	Starch
0	Fruits + Veg
0	Milk 1%
1	Sugars
3	Protein
3	Fat
0	Extras

Prep Time

Roast Chicken

Chicken Burritos with Salad

Instructions:

Don't change yet! Take out equipment.

1. Preheat oven to 350º F.

   Heat oil in a large nonstick fry pan or wok at med-high.

   Cut chicken into bite size pieces and gradually add to pan as you cut. Stir until no longer pink.

   Add sour cream, chilies and cheeses to <u>cooked meat</u> and stir. Remove from heat.

   Spray a large cake pan with cooking spray.

   Distribute chicken mixture on centre of tortillas.

   Roll up tortillas, folding the sides under, to ensure that filling does not run out. Carefully place burritos inside the pan, sprinkle with cheeses, <u>cover</u> pan with foil and bake in **hot oven**. Set timer for 20 minutes.

2. Chop lettuce into salad spinner, spin dry and arrange on plates.

   Cube tomatoes and slice green onions. Sprinkle on top of lettuce and drizzle with dressing.

   My family loves fat-free sour cream and extra salsa on the side.

Ingredients:

Take out ingredients.

1 tsp canola or olive oil.

3 boneless skinless chicken breasts (approx 450 g)

1 cup fat-free sour cream
1 can (127 mL) chopped green chilies (Old El Paso)
1/2 cup <u>each</u> of <u>grated low-fat Monterey Jack</u> and <u>grated low-fat Cheddar cheese</u>

cooking spray (no-cholesterol)

8 large flour tortillas (Old El Paso)

**1/2 cup <u>each</u>, <u>grated low-fat Monterey Jack</u> and <u>grated low-fat Cheddar cheeses</u>
aluminum foil**

1 head lettuce

2 Roma tomatoes
4 green onions
3 Tbsp of your favorite low-cal dressing

fat-free sour cream (optional)
chunky salsa (optional)

<u>**Serves 4-6**</u>

Eating Time

Equipment List:

Lge nonstick fry pan or wok
Rectangular cake pan
Aluminum foil
Salad spinner
Cutting board
Sharp meat knife
Sharp veggie knife
Can opener
Lge mixing spoon
Measuring cups & spoons

Per serving:

Calories	360
Fat	11.1 g
Protein	32.9 g
Carbohydrate	32.3 g

Food Choices:

1 1/2	Starch
0	Fruits + Veg
1/2	Milk 1%
1/2	Sugars
4	Protein
1 1/2	Fat
0	Extras

Prep Time

Chicken Burritos

Chinese Beef Stir-Fry with Rice

Instructions:

Don't change yet! Take out equipment.

1. Combine rice and water in a microwave-safe pot or casserole dish with lid. <u>Cover</u> and **microwave** at high. Set timer for 20-25 minutes.

2. Heat oil in a large nonstick fry pan or wok at med-high.

   Cut beef into thin strips and add to pan as you cut. Brown until meat is no longer pink. Add pepper to taste.

   Chop onion, zucchini and peppers into bite size chunks, in that order. Add to meat pan as you chop. Toss occasionally while completing the next step.

   Combine in a small bowl, in this order; cornstarch, gradually whisk in broth, black bean sauce, brown sugar and chilies. Add sauce to meat pan. Leave at a high simmer until it starts to thicken a little. <u>Reduce heat</u> and let simmer until rice is ready.

3. Rice should be ready now so lift with a fork, then <u>return lid</u>. Place on table to set for 5 minutes while setting the table.

Ingredients:

Take out ingredients.

1-1/2 cups white rice (Uncle Ben's Brand)
3 cups water

1 tsp canola or olive oil

450 g sirloin steak (boneless & trimmed)
fresh ground pepper

1 onion
1 zucchini
1 small green pepper
1 small red pepper

2-1/2 Tbsp cornstarch
1 can (284 mL) beef broth (Campbell's)
4 Tbsp black bean sauce
1 Tbsp brown sugar
1/8 tsp dry crushed chilies
Add more chilies if you like spicy food.

Serves 4-6

Eating Time

Equipment List:

Lge nonstick fry pan or wok
Lge microwave-safe pot w/lid
Small bowl
Cutting board
Sharp meat knife
Sharp veggie knife
Can opener
Small & lge mixing spoons
Measuring cups & spoons

Per serving:

Calories	332
Fat	5.8 g
Protein	21.9 g
Carbohydrate	48.1 g

Food Choices:

2 1/2	Starch
1/2	Fruits + Veg
0	Milk 1%
1/2	Sugars
2 1/2	Protein
1/2	Fat
0	Extras

Prep Time

Chinese Beef Stir-Fry

Spinach Lasagna with Bread Rolls

Instructions:

Don't change yet! Take out equipment.

1. Preheat oven to 375º F.
   Heat oil in a large nonstick fry pan or wok at med-high.
   Chop onion (finely) and add to pan as you chop. Add garlic and saute for about 2 minutes, then remove from heat.

   Add cottage cheese and eggs to onion pan and mix together until well blended. Add spinach and spices and stir to complete the **spinach mix**. Set aside.

   Heat oil at med-high in a separate **stove-top pan**. Stir in flour and gradually add milk. Stir until smooth. Add spices and cheeses. Stir until cheese has melted to complete **cheese sauce**. Remove from heat and set aside.

   Spread a few spoons of cheese sauce over the bottom of a rectangular lasagna or cake pan.

   Layer with 1/3 dry noodles, 1/3 spinach mix and 1/3 cheese sauce. Repeat layers **2** more times.

   Sprinkle mozzarella cheese over top of last layer, cover tightly with foil shiny side down and bake in **hot oven**. Set timer for 35 min.

2. Separate bread stick rolls from each other, but do not unroll into sticks. Place rolls on a rectangular cake pan, brush with oil and sprinkle with fines herbs and white sugar. **Set aside**. When timer rings for lasagna, uncover. Leave it in on bottom rack and place your bread rolls in **oven** on top rack. Reset timer for 12-15 minutes or until they are golden brown.

Ingredients:

Take out ingredients.

1 tsp olive oil

1 onion
1 tsp prepared garlic

1 tub (500 mL) 1% cottage cheese
4 large eggs
600 g frozen chopped spinach, thawed and lightly drained
fresh ground pepper to taste
1/8 tsp each of salt & nutmeg

3 Tbsp canola or olive oil
3 Tbsp flour
2 cups 1% milk
fresh ground pepper to taste
1 cup each of grated part-skim mozzarella cheese and grated low-fat Parmesan cheese

12 Catelli Express Oven Ready lasagna noodles

1/2 cup grated part-skim mozzarella cheese
aluminum foil

1 pkg (311 g) Pillsbury bread sticks

1 tsp each of canola oil, fines herbs and white sugar for all the bread rolls

Let the lasagna stand for approx 5 minutes after it has baked, about the time it takes to set the table. This allows it to set.

Serves 6-8

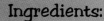

Eating Time

Equipment List:

Cookie sheet
Lge nonstick fry pan or wok
Lasagna or cake pan
Med stove-top pot
Cutting board
Sharp veggie knife
Cheese grater
Pastry brush
Small & lge stirring spoons
Measuring cups & spoons

Per serving:

Calories	498
Fat	18.0 g
Protein	33.1 g
Carbohydrate	50.9 g

Food Choices:

3	Starch
0	Fruits + Veg
1	Milk 1%
0	Sugars
3 1/2	Protein
2	Fat
0	Extras

15

Prep Time

Spinach Lasagna

8

Hazelnut Chicken with Pasta and Salad

Instructions:	Ingredients:
Don't change yet! Take out equipment.	Take out ingredients.

1. Bring water to a boil in a large **stove-top** pot <u>with lid</u>.

   6 L water (approx)

2. Heat oil in a large nonstick fry pan or wok at med-high.

   1 tsp canola or olive oil

   Cut chicken into bite size pieces and gradually add chicken to pan as you cut.

   3 boneless skinless chicken breasts (approx 450 g)

   Stir until meat is no longer pink and reduce heat to med-low.

   Sliver carrot, chop onion, then wash and slice mushrooms in that order, gradually adding to chicken as you cut.

   1 peeled carrot
   3 green onions
   10 mushrooms

   Add to pan in this order: butter, flour and salt. Gradually stir in milk.

   1-1/2 Tbsp butter or margarine
   1-1/2 Tbsp flour
   pinch of salt
   1 cup 1% milk

   Add spice, hazelnut liqueur, lime juice, honey and chili-garlic sauce. Stir. <u>Cover</u> and simmer.

   1/8 tsp coriander
   1-1/2 tsp Mrs. Dash Original Seasoning
   4 Tbsp hazelnut liqueur
   2 Tbsp lime juice
   2 Tbsp liquid honey
   3/4 tsp chili-garlic sauce *You can add more if you like things spicy.*

3. Place pasta in boiling water, stir and cook <u>uncovered</u>. Set timer for 7 min.

   1 pkg (375 g) Catelli Bistro fusilli pasta *Garlic and Parsley*

4. Wash Romaine and tear into bite size pieces into salad spinner. Rinse under cold water and spin dry.

   1 head Romaine lettuce

   Transfer to salad bowl, add croutons and toss with dressing.

   1/2 cup croutons
   3 Tbsp of your favorite low-cal salad dressing

5. Rinse the **cooked** pasta under hot water in a colander.

   <u>Serves 4-6</u>

Eating Time

Equipment List:

Lge stove-top pot w/lid
Lge nonstick fry pan or wok
Salad spinner
Salad bowl
Colander
Cutting board
Sharp meat knife
Sharp veggie knife
Carrot peeler
Lge stirring spoon
Measuring cups & spoons

Per serving:

Calories	446
Fat	6.8 g
Protein	29.6 g
Carbohydrate	66.6 g

Food Choices:

3	Starch
1/2	Fruits + Veg
0	Milk 1%
1 1/2	Sugars
3	Protein
1	Fat
0	Extras

Prep Time

Kitchen Help

DAAAD! I'M ALMOST LATE!!

HEY DAD, YOU JUST DRIVE HER TO JUDO, AND I'LL CLEAN UP THE KITCHEN FOR YOU!!

GEE THANKS! SLAM VROOM

LATER WHERE IS EVERYTHING?

L. BENNETT

Hazelnut Chicken

8

Things You Should Know About the Recipes

Blue

Notice we don't use a bottom crust. On my wish list for this year is that a company who makes a lower-fat delicious pie crust, will make a package with just lids!! For now we will need to put the bottom on the top! Why? Because you double your fat when you double up! Sooo you have to scoop a little...it's worth it! This is fantastic the veggie way by omitting the meat. Once the sauce is in the pie plate cut in cubes of firm tofu, then cover!!!

Yellow Wings

This is a fun, messy meal! I feel like a kid while I'm eating it! It's juuust delicious. This is not my favorite veggie conversion because the soya hamburger replacement doesn't taste quite right with this recipe. If you are an avid vegetarian, however, you can give it a try. It's not bad, but it's not quite up to the standard for taste as all the others.

Red Wings

Oh Oh Oh Oh Oh!! We kinda like this one! Here's an entertaining tip. Instead of pasta...sometimes I make up some instant mashed potatoes, stir in some low-fat grated Parmesan cheese and pepper, then roll a clump in a combination of corn flake crumbs, grated low-fat Cheddar, pepper and Mrs. Dash Original Seasoning. Pop these in a hot 375° F oven in a nonstick muffin tin for about 25 minutes or until they get crunchy. Serve this beside the chicken with toasted almonds scattered on top and I guarantee a reaction! What do I do with the left over cherries? You can either freeze them for the next time ooor you can make a paste with 2 Tbsp each cornstarch, sugar and water in a stove-top pot, add the cherries and cook on med-high heat until it thickens. This makes an amazing ice cream topper sometime during the week!

Green

This is a great way to enjoy ribs without the fuss, the fat or the mess! Rated as a favorite amongst our families!

Yellow

This is an amazing stir-fry. The cashews really add a nice touch to this meal. Simply omit the meat step at the beginning if you are a veggie lover. This is absolutely delicious with chunks of firm tofu thrown in instead.

Week 9

Blue: Sirloin Pepper Steak Pie
with Baked Vegetables

> Our Family Rating: 8
> Your Family Rating: _____

Yellow Wings: Hard Shell Tacos with Fixn's

> Our Family Rating: 10
> Your Family Rating: _____

Red Wings: French Cherry Chicken with Pasta
and Green Beans

> Our family Rating 10
> Your Family Rating ___

Green: Beefy Boneless Sticky Ribs They're Not,
with Rice and Snow Peas

> Our Family Rating: 9
> Your Family Rating: _____

Yellow: Spicy Stir-Fry Chicken with Rice

> Our Family Rating: 10
> Your Family Rating: _____

9

Sirloin Pepper Steak Pie
with Baked Vegetables

Instructions:

Don't change yet! **Take pie crust out to thaw first**, then take out equipment.

1. Preheat oven to 375° F.

   Heat oil in a large nonstick wok or fry pan at med-high.

   Cut meat into small bite size cubes and add to pan as you chop.

   Cut onion and peppers into medium chunks, in that order, and add to meat pan as you chop. Stir.

   Wash and slice mushrooms and add to meat pan. Stir.

   Add soup and Worcestershire to meat and stir until well blended. Pour meat sauce into <u>empty pie plate</u> with NO BOTTOM CRUST. <u>Cover</u> with thawed crust and seal all edges. It looks all messy when you put the top on but don't worry. It turns out great once baked. Bake in **hot oven**. Set timer for 40 minutes.

2. Cut tomatoes and zucchini in thick slices and place on cookie sheet. Drizzle with oil and sprinkle with spices.

   Bake in **hot oven** beside meat pie. When timer rings, both are ready. Make sure pie crust is nicely browned.

   Remember *Let the pie stand for about 5 minutes to set, while you're setting the table.*

Ingredients:

Take out ingredients.
1 lower-fat deep dish frozen pie crust

1 tsp canola or olive oil

350 g sirloin beef steak (boneless and trimmed)

1 onion
1 small green pepper

7 mushrooms

1 can (284 mL) Campbell's Golden Mushroom Soup
1 Tbsp Worcestershire sauce

4 Roma tomatoes
1 small zucchini
1 Tbsp olive oil
or use an olive oil spray to cut down fat
1 tsp Italian seasoning
fresh ground pepper to taste
salt (optional)

Optional *Ketchup for the kids!!!*

<u>Serves 4-6</u>

55

Eating Time

Equipment List:

Take out pie crust
Pie plate
Cookie sheet w/edges
Lge nonstick fry pan or wok
Cutting board
Sharp meat knife
Sharp veggie knife
Can opener
Lge stirring spoon
Measuring spoons

Per serving:

Calories	308
Fat	14.6 g
Protein	17.5 g
Carbohydrate	26.7 g

Food Choices:

1	Starch
1/2	Fruits + Veg
0	Milk 1%
1/2	Sugars
2	Protein
2	Fat
0	Extras

20

Prep Time

Sirloin Pepper Steak Pie

Hard Shell Tacos with Fixn's

Instructions:

Don't change yet! Take out equipment.

1. Preheat oven to 400° F.

2. Brown meat in large nonstick pan at med-high until no longer red. Add spices while meat is browning.

    Add ketchup and water after meat has browned. Simmer.

3. Spray cookie sheet with cooking spray. Place fries on sheet, spray the tops and **bake** 15-20 minutes or until golden brown. Turn once.

4. Shred lettuce into basket of salad spinner, rinse and spin dry.

    Chop green onion and slice tomatoes.

    Arrange vegetables on serving platter with sour cream, salsa and grated cheese.

5. Spoon 2-3 Tbsp of meat mixture into each taco and sprinkle with cheese.

    Add whatever your little heart desires off the serving platter!!

If you want to make the French fries or potato puffs more like a restaurant's, just sprinkle with Cajun seasoning or seasoning salt.

Ingredients:

Take out ingredients.

450 g ground beef (90% lean)
2 tsp chili powder
1 tsp cumin powder
1/4 tsp turmeric
2 tsp onion flakes

1/2 cup <u>each</u> of <u>ketchup</u> and <u>water</u>

cooking spray (no-cholesterol)
500 g frozen French fries (McCain's)
or 3-4 cups frozen potato puffs as shown

1/3 head lettuce

4 green onions
4 Roma tomatoes

1/2 cup <u>each</u> of <u>fat-free sour cream</u> and <u>chunky salsa</u>
3/4 cup grated low-fat Cheddar cheese (for all)

1 pkg (12) hard shell tacos (Old El Paso)

Cajun seasoning or seasoning salt (optional)

<u>Serves 4-6</u>

Eating Time

Equipment List:

Lge nonstick fry pan or wok
Lge stove-top pot w/lid
Med microwave-safe pot w/lid
Mixing bowl
Colander
Cutting board
Sharp meat knife
Can opener
Lge mixing spoon
Measuring cups & spoons

Per serving:

Calories	432
Fat	4.3 g
Protein	34.6 g
Carbohydrate	63.8 g

Food Choices:

2 1/2	Starch
1	Fruits + Veg
0	Milk 1%
1 1/2	Sugars
4	Protein
1/2	Fat
0	Extras

Prep Time

Food Fight

French Cherry Chicken

9

Beefy Boneless Sticky Ribs They're Not, with Rice and Snow Peas

Instructions:

Don't change yet! Take out equipment.

1. Preheat oven to 375° F.
   Cut meat into 1/2" thick rectangular strips.
   Place meat in oven-safe pan or casserole dish
   with lid. Sprinkle with garlic powder.

   Mix ketchup, salsa and brown sugar in a small
   mixing bowl. Pour over meat.

   Chop 1 stalk of celery (finely) and sprinkle
   over top. <u>Cover</u> and place in **hot oven**. Set
   timer for 55 minutes.

2. Combine rice and water in a different oven-
   safe casserole dish with lid. <u>Cover</u> and place
   in **hot oven** beside meat. When timer rings,
   both meat and rice are ready.

3. Rinse snow peas under cold water in a
   colander. Place in small fry pan. Add butter,
   soya sauce and thyme. Let stand.

   Stir-fry snow peas at high for a few minutes
   until hot, <u>just before serving</u>.

Ingredients:

Take out ingredients.

**675 g sirloin beef steak (boneless and
trimmed)**
1 tsp garlic powder

1 cup ketchup
1/4 cup chunky salsa
1/2 cup brown sugar

1 stalk celery

1-1/2 cups white rice (Uncle Ben's Brand)
3 cups water

1 pkg (approx 200 g) frozen snow peas
1 tsp butter or margarine
1 tsp soya sauce
pinch of <u>dried</u> thyme leaves (not ground)

<u>Serves 4-6</u>

Eating Time

Equipment List:

Lge oven-safe pot w/lid
Oven safe pot or casserole w/lid
Small fry pan
Small mixing bowl
Colander
Cutting board
Sharp meat knife
Sharp veggie knife
Lge mixing spoon
Measuring cups & spoons

Per serving:

Calories	449
Fat	7.2 g
Protein	30.1 g
Carbohydrate	65.8 g

Food Choices:

2	Starch
1/2	Fruits + Veg
0	Milk 1%
3	Sugars
3 1/2	Protein
1/2	Fat
0	Extras

15

Prep Time

Beefy Boneless Sticky Ribs

Spicy Stir-Fry Chicken with Rice

Instructions:

Don't change yet! Take out equipment.

1. Combine rice and water in a large microwave-safe pot with lid. <u>Cover</u> and **microwave** on high. Set timer for 20-25 minutes.

2. Heat oil in a large nonstick wok or fry pan at med-high.

   Cut chicken into bite size pieces and add gradually to pan as you cut.

   Sliver onion, chop peppers in chunks and slice mushrooms in that order. Add to pan as you cut and stir-fry for 2-3 minutes (see page 20 for fast cutting tips).

   Combine, in this order, in a small bowl; cornstarch, gradually stir in ketchup until smooth and not lumpy, chicken broth, soya sauce, brown sugar, garlic and curry. Stir well to make **sauce** and let stand.

   Cut tomato into cubes and add **sauce** and tomatoes to chicken pan. Stir, bring to a boil, then reduce heat to a simmer until timer rings for rice. *Remember to let rice stand about 5 minutes while setting the table.*

   Serve sauce on the rice and sprinkle with cashew nuts.

Ingredients:

Take out ingredients.

1-1/2 cups white rice (Uncle Ben's Brand)
3 cups water

1 tsp canola or extra virgin olive oil

3 boneless skinless chicken breasts (approx 450 g)

1 small onion
1 small green pepper
1 small red pepper
10 fresh mushrooms (washed)

2-1/2 Tbsp cornstarch
1/2 cup hot ketchup
If you like spicy food add some chili-garlic sauce to this step.
1 can (284 mL) chicken broth (Campbell's)
3 Tbsp <u>each</u> of <u>soya sauce</u> and <u>brown sugar</u>
1 tsp prepared garlic
2 tsp curry powder

2 firm Roma tomatoes

1/3 cup cashew nuts (*optional... but extremely nummy. In fact, it would be a shame if you leave them out!....buuut, don't let me make up your mind...sort of.*)

<u>Serves 4-6</u>

30
Eating Time

Equipment List:

Lge nonstick wok or fry pan
Lge microwave-safe pot w/lid
Small mixing bowl
Cutting board
Sharp meat knife
Sharp veggie knife
Can opener
Lge stirring spoon
Measuring cups & spoons

Per serving:

Calories	364
Fat	3.2 g
Protein	26.1 g
Carbohydrate	57.7 g

Food Choices:

2 1/2	Starch
1/2	Fruits + Veg
0	Milk 1%
1 1/2	Sugars
3	Protein
1/2	Fat
0	Extras

Prep Time

Spicy Stir-Fry Chicken

Things You Should Know About the Recipes

Blue

This is by far my favorite type of hamburger. Some of my kids don't like the pineapple slice. Some like to eat it separate. I looove it on! The sauce you drizzle on top is amazing! These are drippy, sloppy and veeery tasty!!!

Yellow Wings

When the test families got their hands on this recipe, they couldn't believe they ever bought boxed. Check out the nutritional data on this meal! It's like you're eating junk food when you're not!
Note: Don't over cook your chicken or it gets dry!

Red Wings

I usually serve the peppercorn sauce on the side in a gravy boat. Some of our kids prefer to have their steak lathered with steak sauce or ketchup, others like a little on the side, some of us...like me, just can't get enough. The side is the safest bet!

Green

You want to be home while this is cooking so you can baste it occasionally! NUMMY! NUMMY! NUMMY! NUMMY and did I mention NUMMY!!! ...and the only reason this didn't get a 10 rating with our family is because we have two children who seem to think only pasta and potatoes should have been discovered!!

Yellow Wings

This is a fantastic pasta sauce whether you leave out the meat or not! You can fry up firm tofu with this for protein. It is designed to suit all kinds of taste buds so if you're a spicy food person just kick up the heat with extra chili sauce!!!

Week 10

Blue: Lean Teriyaki Hawaiian Burgers
                             with Papaya Salad

> Our family rating: 10
> Your family rating: _____

Yellow Wings   Baked Chicken Fingers
                             with Spinach Salad

> Our family rating: 9.5
> Your family rating: _____

Red Wings: Peppercorn Steak with Rice
                             and Baby Carrots

> Our family rating: 8.5
> Your family rating: _____

Green: Honey-Curried Chicken with Rice
                             and Oriental Vegetables

> Our family rating: 9.5
> Your family rating: _____

Yellow Wings: Szechuan Orange-Ginger Chicken
                             with Pasta & Vegetables

> Our family rating: 10
> Your family rating _____

10

Lean Teriyaki Hawaiian Burgers with Papaya Salad

Instructions:

Don't change yet! Take out equipment.

1. Preheat oven to 350º F.

   Shape meat into six thick patties and arrange in an oven-safe cake pan or casserole dish.

   Chop green onion and sprinkle over burgers.

   Pour teriyaki sauce over burgers. Top each burger with one slice of pineapple. Bake in **hot oven**. Set timer for 50 minutes.

2. Chop onion (finely).

   Peel papaya, remove seeds and set aside for dressing. Cut papaya into bite size pieces. *You can also add some chopped avocado if you like.*

   Tear lettuce into bite size pieces into salad spinner. Rinse under cold water and spin dry. **Refrigerate** in a bowl until ready.

   Salad Dressing
   Combine vinegar, sugar, mustard, salt and papaya seeds in a small bowl. Let stand in **fridge**.

3. Combine cornstarch and (gradually stir in) pineapple juice in a small **stove-top** pot. Stir until well blended and let stand.

   ...when timer rings for burgers...
   Add teriyaki drippings from pan, to the pineapple juice pot and bring to a boil. Stir until thickened. This sauce is to pour over the burger before putting the top of the bun on.

4. Drizzle the salad dressing all over salad and toss until coated.

Ingredients:

Take out ingredients.

675 g ground beef (90% lean)

3 green onions

1 cup bottled teriyaki sauce or marinade
1 can (398 mL) pineapple slices (reserve light syrup)

1 small onion

1 small papaya (approx 350 g)
1 small avocado (optional)

1 head lettuce

1/3 cup white wine vinegar
1/4 cup white sugar
3/4 tsp each of dried mustard and salt
3 tsp papaya seeds (optional)

1 Tbsp cornstarch
1/2 cup reserved pineapple juice (from the can)

1 cup of teriyaki drippings

6 hamburger buns

Serves 4-6

55

Eating Time

Equipment List:

Cake pan or casserole dish
Small stove-top pot
Small bowl
Salad bowl
Salad spinner
Cutting board
Sharp veggie knife
Can opener
Small mixing spoon
Measuring cups & spoons

Per serving:

Calories	562
Fat	20.7 g
Protein	30.3 g
Carbohydrate	63.6 g

Food Choices:

2	Starch
1 1/2	Fruit + Veg
0	Milk 1%
2	Sugars
3 1/2	Protein
2 1/2	Fat
0	Extras

Prep Time

Lean Teriyaki Hawaiian Burgers

Baked Chicken Fingers with Spinach Salad

Instructions:

Don't change yet! Take out equipment.

1. Preheat oven to 375° F.

    Cut chicken into long strips.
    Beat egg white and milk in a bowl and toss in the chicken. Stir to coat.

    Mix together corn flake crumbs and spices in a different bowl.

    Spray a cookie sheet with cooking spray.

    Dunk each piece of chicken in the crumbs using a fork. Arrange on a cookie sheet. Spray the tops with cooking spray and place in **hot oven**. Set timer for 20 minutes.

    Combine sour cream, mayonnaise and curry in a bowl. Stir together until smooth. Set this curry dip aside in **fridge**.

2. Cut stems from spinach and break into bite size pieces into salad spinner. Rinse under cold water and spin dry.
    Wash and slice mushrooms.

    Combine spinach and mushrooms in a salad bowl. Sprinkle with croutons and bacon bits.

    Mix together mayonnaise, Italian dressing and sugar in a small cup or bowl. Pour dressing over salad **just before serving**. Toss to coat.

3. The curry mayonnaise sauce is for dipping the chicken fingers in. You can also serve them with plum sauce.
    Our family likes both for the variety!

Ingredients:

Take out ingredients.

4 large boneless skinless chicken breasts (approx 700 g)
1 egg white mixed with 3 Tbsp 1% milk

1 cup corn flake crumbs
1 tsp Mrs. Dash Original Seasoning
1 tsp fresh ground pepper

cooking spray (no-cholesterol)

If you like spicy chicken fingers you can use blackened cajun spice instead of fresh ground pepper.

Curry Sauce for Dipping
1/4 cup each fat-free sour cream and lowest-fat mayonnaise
1/2 tsp curry powder

1 bunch fresh spinach

8 mushrooms

1/2 cup croutons
2 Tbsp real bacon bits (packaged)

2 Tbsp each of lowest-fat mayonnaise and low-cal Italian dressing
1 tsp white sugar
garnish salad with low-fat Cheddar cheese (optional)

1 jar (227 mL) V-H plum sauce (optional)

Serves 4-6

25

Eating Time

Equipment List:

Cookie sheet w/edges
4 small bowls
Salad bowl
Salad spinner
Cutting board
Sharp meat knife
Sharp veggie knife
Fork
Small mixing spoon
Measuring cups & spoon

Per serving:

Calories	260
Fat	4.2 g
Protein	32.5 g
Carbohydrate	23.2 g

Food Choices:

1	Starch
0	Fruit + Veg
0	Milk 1%
1	Sugars
4 1/2	Protein
1/2	Fat
0	Extras

Prep Time

Baked Chicken Fingers

10

143

Peppercorn Steak with Rice and Baby Carrots

Instructions:

Don't change yet! Take out equipment.

1. Combine rice and water in a microwave-safe pot or casserole dish with lid. <u>Cover</u> and **microwave** at high for 20-25 minutes.

2. Prepare sauce according to package directions in a small **stove-top** pot. Simmer.

3. Bring water and carrots to a boil in a small **stove-top** pot. Reduce heat, stir and simmer.

4. Spray a large nonstick fry pan with cooking spray. Brown one side of steak at med-high.

...meanwhile...
Chop green onions, then wash and slice mushrooms.

Flip meat over to brown other side and toss in mushrooms and onion. <u>Reduce heat</u> until rice is ready.

5. Drain carrots when they are are tender and mix in white sugar and spice. Stir.

The peppercorn sauce is meant to be served over top of the steak on each individual plate. Some of my kids like the peppercorn sauce served on the side. You may want to leave it as an option and put the sauce in a gravy boat.

Ingredients:

Take out ingredients.

1-1/2 cups white rice (Uncle Ben's Brand)
3 cups water

1 pkg peppercorn sauce (dry mix)
(approx 40 g)
*you will need **1% milk** for this*

1 pkg (500 g) frozen baby carrots
(Green Giant)
1/4 cup water

cooking spray (no-cholesterol)
675 g sirloin steak (boneless and trimmed)

2 green onion
7 mushrooms

1 tsp white sugar
1/2 tsp Mrs. Dash Original Seasoning

<u>Serves 4-6</u>

25

Eating Time

144

Equipment List:

Lge nonstick fry pan
Lge microwave-safe pot w/lid
2 small stove-top pots
Cutting board
Sharp veggie knife
Fork
Measuring cups & spoons

Per serving:

Calories	395
Fat	7.8 g
Protein	31.4 g
Carbohydrate	49.8 g

Food Choices:

2	Starch
1	Fruit + Veg
0	Milk 1%
1	Sugars
3 1/2	Protein
0	Fat
0	Extras

Prep Time

Peppercorn Steak

10

Honey-Curried Chicken with Rice and Oriental Vegetables

Instructions:

Don't change yet! Take out equipment.

1. Preheat oven to 375° F.

    Unravel thighs to flatten and scrunch together in a square <u>oven-safe</u> baking dish or pan, <u>uncovered</u>.

    Mix together honey, mustard and spices in a bowl. Pour sauce over chicken.

    Sprinkle with tarragon leaves.

    Bake in **hot oven**. Set timer for 50 minutes.

    Baste occasionally if you can.

2. Combine rice and water in an <u>oven-safe</u> pot with lid.

    <u>Cover</u> and cook in **hot oven** beside chicken. When timer rings, both chicken and rice are ready.

3. Rinse vegetables in colander under cold water. Place in a medium size microwave-safe pot or casserole dish with lid. <u>Cover</u> and **microwave** at high for 5 minutes, then let stand.

    Microwave vegetables at high for 2 additional minutes <u>just before serving</u>. Add salt and butter if you must.

Ingredients:

Take out your ingredients.

8-12 boneless skinless chicken thighs (approx 800 g) *or chicken legs, as shown*

1/2 cup liquid honey
1/4 cup prepared mustard
1 tsp curry powder
1/4 tsp salt

1/2 tsp dried tarragon leaves

1-1/2 cups white rice (Uncle Ben's Brand)
3 cups water

1 pkg (500 g) Green Giant Oriental Style frozen vegetables

1/4 tsp salt (optional)
butter or margarine (optional)

<u>Serves 4-6</u>

55

Eating Time

Equipment List:

Square oven-safe pan
Lge oven-safe pot w/lid
Microwave-safe pot w/lid
Colander
Mixing bowl
Lge mixing spoon
Measuring cups & spoons

Per serving:

Calories	441
Fat	6.5 g
Protein	32.2 g
Carbohydrate	63.4 g

Food Choices:

2	Starch
1/2	Fruit + Veg
0	Milk 1%
3	Sugars
4	Protein
0	Fat
0	Extras

15

Prep Time

Honey-Curried Chicken

10

Szechuan Orange-Ginger Chicken with Pasta and Vegetables

Instructions:	Ingredients:
Don't change yet! Take out equipment.	Take out ingredients.

Instructions:

Don't change yet! Take out equipment.

1. Bring water to a boil in a large **stove-top** pot <u>with lid</u> at high.

2. Heat oil in a large nonstick fry pan or wok at med-high.

   Cut chicken into bite size pieces and gradually add to pan as you cut. Stir until meat is no longer pink.

   Combine in this order, in a small bowl; tahini, dry-garlic sauce, orange juice, chili sauce, sherry, garlic, ginger, brown sugar and cumin. Stir together and pour over chicken.   Stir and lower heat to high simmer.

   Sliver red pepper and add to chicken. Stir.

3. Rinse vegetables in colander under cold water. Place in a medium size microwave-safe pot or casserole dish <u>with lid</u>. **Microwave** at high for 5 minutes, then let stand.

4. Place pasta in boiling water and set timer for 4 minutes.

5. Add spice to vegetables and **microwave** at high for 2 additional minutes <u>just before serving</u>. (When they are done you may add a little butter if you must.)

The sauce is meant to be poured over the individual servings of pasta. My family looove this dish with crunchy chow mein noodles and peanuts scattered on top. Nuuuuuum!!!!

Ingredients:

Take out ingredients.

6 L water (approx)

1 tsp canola or olive oil

3 boneless skinless chicken breasts (approx 450 g)

2 Tbsp tahini *(ground sesame seeds, looks like peanut butter)*
1/4 cup V-H dry-garlic sauce
1/2 cup orange juice
2 tsp bottled chili-garlic sauce *If you like it really spicy add more chili sauce.*
1/4 cup sherry *(or...combine 1/4 cup red wine and 1 Tbsp brown sugar, mix well)*
2 tsp <u>each</u> of <u>prepared garlic</u>, <u>brown sugar</u> and <u>ground ginger</u>
1 tsp ground cumin

1/2 red pepper (or 1 small)

1 pkg (500 g) cut broccoli (Green Giant)

350 g vermicelli pasta (Catelli)

1 tsp Mrs. Dash Original Seasoning
butter or margarine (optional)

chow mein noodles (optional)
salted peanuts (optional)

<u>Serves 4-6</u>

Eating Time

Equipment List:

Lge nonstick fry pan or wok
Lge stove-top pot w/lid
Microwave-safe pot w/lid
Colander
Small mixing bowl
Cutting board
Sharp veggie knife
Sharp meat knife
Pasta fork
Small & lge mixing spoons
Measuring cups & spoons

Per serving:

Calories	389
Fat	5.4 g
Protein	27.9 g
Carbohydrate	57.2 g

Food Choices:

3	Starch
1/2	Fruit + Veg
0	Milk 1%
1	Sugars
3	Protein
1	Fat
0	Extras

Prep Time

20

Memories

MOM AND DAD, **DON'T** COME OUT OF YOUR ROOM - WE'RE MAKING YOU **BREAKFAST!**

UH, THANKS!! THAT'S SO SWEET!

WE'LL LEAVE YOU ALONE NOW!

SLAM!

HEE HEE

GIGGLE!

BLAAAH! IKK! GAG!!

WE SHOULD HAVE SAID WE WEREN'T HUNGRY!

L. BENNETT

Szechuan Orange-Ginger Chicken

10

Things You Should Know About the Recipes

Yellow

Even if you end up scooping the stuffing off the top of these after they are cooked (because you're not a stuffing person like some members of our family), I think you will enjoy the flavor with or without it. The stuffing spices go through the chop and make them very tasty and very tender!

Blue

This is a delicious meat free supper if you leave out the bacon bits! We love this quiche and it's so fast!

Red Wings

This is sooo fast and sooo delicious and is a fantastic entertaining dish! If you are making this vegetarian style, omit the meat, follow the recipe and add chunks of firm tofu to the sauce while the pasta is cooking.

Green

This is a really unusual chicken recipe. It doesn't look anything like the picture at first and you may think there is a problem ...there's not! Baste the chicken often. and eventually the sauce boils right into the chicken. The paprika adds this almost salty flavor. It has the same effect as potato chips, you can't stop eating!

Yellow Wings

This is not your average pizza. My kids thought it was weird at first but its turned into a family hit!! Take off the dry salami and you've got a great veggie dish!

Week 11

Yellow: Right Side Up Stuffed Mushroom Chops
with Mashed Potatoes and Vegetables

> Our family rating: 9
> Your family rating: _____

Blue: Zippy Quiche with Tossed Salad

> Our family rating: 8
> Your family rating: _____

Red Wings: Chunky Chicken Bengalia with
Pasta and Vegetables

> Our family rating: 10
> Your family rating: _____

Green: Paprika Chicken with Rice
and Green Beans

> Our family rating: 9.5
> Your family rating: _____

Yellow Wings: Hogtown Pizza with Salad Greens

> Our family rating: 8.5
> Your family rating: _____

Right Side Up Stuffed Mushroom Chops with Mashed Potatoes and Vegetables

Instructions:

Don't change yet! Take out equipment.

1. Preheat oven to broil.
   Place chops on a large oven-safe cake pan and **broil** at close range about 1 minute per side.

   ...meanwhile...
   Prepare stuffing in a medium size **stove-top** pot according to package directions, however, **add brown sugar**.

   Remove chops from oven. Drain excess grease from pan. <u>**Re-set oven temperature to 350° F**</u>. Return chops to pan. Mound stuffing on top of each pork chop.

   Combine in this order <u>in the used stuffing pot</u> (**no heat**): soup, gradually stir in water and Worcestershire sauce. Stir until well blended and spoon equally over stuffed chops. Bake in **hot oven**. Set timer for 25 minutes.

2. Boil water in a kettle for the potatoes.

3. Rinse vegetables in colander under cold water. Place in a small microwave-safe pot or casserole dish with lid. <u>Cover</u> and **microwave** at high for 5 minutes, then let stand.

4. Prepare mashed potatoes according to package directions in an <u>oven-safe</u> casserole dish <u>with lid</u>. Always start with liquids and end with flakes. *We use half the required butter.* <u>Cover</u> the potatoes and toss in the **oven** beside the chops. When timer rings, both potatoes and chops are ready.

   Microwave vegetables at high for 2 additional minutes <u>just before serving</u>. Add salt and butter if you must.

Ingredients:

Take out ingredients.

8 pork chops medium thickness boneless and trimmed (approx 700 g)

1 pkg (120 g) Uncle Ben's Stuff'N Such *Traditional Sage*
1 Tbsp brown sugar

1 can (284 mL) cream of mushroom soup (Campbell's)
1/3 soup can water
2 Tbsp Worcestershire sauce

2-1/2 cups water (to allow for boil down)

1 pkg (300 g) frozen mixed vegetables (Green Giant)

1-1/2 cups instant potato flakes (McCain)
*remember to have **1 % milk** and **butter** on hand*

1/8 tsp salt (optional)
butter or margarine (optional)

<u>Serves 4-6</u>

Eating Time

Equipment List:

Oven-safe cake pan
Oven-safe casserole w/lid
Med size stove-top pot
Small microwave-safe pot w/lid
Kettle
Colander
Can opener
Lge mixing spoon
Measuring cups & spoons

Per serving:

Calories	427
Fat	14.5 g
Protein	32.3 g
Carbohydrate	41.9 g

Food Choices:

2	Starch
1/2	Fruit + Veg
0	Milk 1%
1/2	Sugars
4	Protein
1 1/2	Fat
1	Extras

Prep Time

Right Side Up Stuffed Mushroom Chops

11

Zippy Quiche with Tossed Salad

Instructions:

Don't change yet! Take out equipment.

Take one pie crust out first, to let thaw at room temperature. NOW take out equipment.

1. Preheat oven to 375° F.

   Grate and sprinkle cheese into the bottom of pie crust.

   Whip <u>egg whites</u> until frothy in a mixing bowl. <u>Add yolks</u>, milk and pepper. Mix together until well blended.

   Pour into pie crust over first layer of cheese.

   Spray a large nonstick fry pan with cooking spray. Place at med-high heat.

   Chop onion, green pepper and mushrooms and add to pan as you chop. Saute about 1 minute.

   Add to pie crust in this order; sauteed vegetables, bacon bits and top with balance of cheese.

   Bake in **hot oven**. Set timer for 50 minutes until top is golden brown and inserted knife comes clean.

2. Tear lettuce into bite size pieces into salad spinner. Rinse under cold water and spin dry. **Refrigerate** in a bowl until ready.

3. Wash an apple <u>just before serving</u>. Cut into 1/4's, cut off core, then cut into bite size chunks. Add to salad bowl. Pour dressing over salad and toss to coat <u>just before serving</u>.

Ingredients:

Take out ingredients.

1 deep dish lower-fat frozen pie shell

1/2 cup grated low-fat Cheddar cheese

5 large eggs
1/2 cup 1% milk
fresh ground pepper to taste

cooking spray (no-cholesterol)

1 small onion
1/2 small green pepper
10 mushrooms

2 Tbsp real bacon bits (packaged)
1 cup grated low-fat Cheddar cheese

1 head green leaf lettuce

1 apple (unpeeled)

3 Tbsp low-cal creamy Italian dressing

croutons are delicious with this salad (optional)

<u>**Serves 4-6**</u>

60

Eating Time

Equipment List:

Take pie crust out
Pie plate
Nonstick fry pan
Salad spinner
Salad bowl
Mixing bowl
Cheese grater
Cutting board
Sharp veggie knife
Fork
Lge mixing spoon
Measuring cups & spoons

Per serving:

Calories	293
Fat	13.9 g
Protein	15.7 g
Carbohydrate	26.3 g

Food Choices:

1	Starch
1	Fruit + Veg
0	Milk 1%
0	Sugars
2	Protein
2	Fat
0	Extras

Prep Time

Zippy Quiche

11

Chunky Chicken Bengalia
with Pasta and Vegetables

Instructions:

Don't change yet! Take out equipment.

1. Heat oil in a large nonstick fry pan or wok at med-high.

   Cut chicken into bite size pieces and gradually add to pan as you cut. Stir until meat is no longer pink. Add curry while meat is browning.

   Wash and slice mushrooms and add to meat pan as you cut.

2. Bring a large <u>covered</u> pot of water to a boil.

3. Rinse broccoli in a colander under cold water. Place in microwave-safe pot or casserole dish with lid. <u>Cover</u> and **microwave** at high for 5 minutes, then let stand.

4. Add salsa and peach jam to the chicken pan. Stir until well blended. Let simmer until pasta is ready to serve.

5. Add pasta to boiling water and set timer for 11 minutes.

   Rinse **cooked** pasta in a colander. Return to pot (no heat). Toss with basil and a little olive oil if you wish.

6. Add spice to the vegetable, <u>return cover</u> and cook an additional 2 minutes <u>just before serving</u>. Stir in a little butter if you must.

I use to serve a little spoon of this sauce on the side of the pasta because my kids thought it looked disgusting! This is now a family favorite...to say the least!

Ingredients:

Take out ingredients.

1 tsp canola or olive oil

3 boneless skinless chicken breasts (approx 450 g)
1/2 Tbsp curry powder

12 fresh mushrooms

6 L water (approx)

1 pkg (500 g) frozen cut broccoli (Green Giant)

3 cups chunky salsa
3 Tbsp (heaping) peach jam

1 pkg (375 g) Catelli Bistro fettuccini pasta *Italian Herb*

1/2 tsp basil
olive oil (optional)

Mrs. Dash Original Seasoning to taste

1 tsp butter (optional)
grated low-fat Parmesan cheese (optional)

<u>Serves 4-6</u>

Eating Time

Equipment List:

Lge nonstick fry pan or wok
Lge stove-top pot w/lid
Med microwave-safe pot w/lid
Colander
Cutting board
Sharp meat knife
Sharp veggie knife
Pasta fork
Lge mixing spoon
Measuring cups & spoons

Per serving:

Calories	451
Fat	6.6 g
Protein	31.5 g
Carbohydrate	66.2 g

Food Choices:

3	Starch
1	Fruit + Veg
0	Milk 1%
1	Sugars
3 1/2	Protein
1	Fat
0	Extras

Prep Time

— Kid Table Talk —

Chunky Chicken Bengalia

Paprika Chicken with Rice and Green Beans

Instructions:

Don't change yet! Take out equipment.

1. Preheat oven to 350° F.

2. Spray a large nonstick fry pan with cooking spray and brown chicken at med-high. Brown all sides. *I use my electric fry pan.*

   Chop onion (finely) and add to pan as you cut. Add garlic and saute about 1 minute.

   Add broth and spices to browned chicken and stir. Bring to a boil and <u>cover</u>. Reduce heat to med-low for a high simmer. Set timer for 45 minutes.

   Baste occasionally if you can. **The liquids end up boiling into the chicken. It does not make a sauce - It just makes the chicken itself saucy.**

3. Combine rice and water in an <u>oven-safe</u> pot with lid. <u>Cover</u> and cook in **hot oven.**

4. Heat oil <u>in a different</u> nonstick fry pan at med-high.

   Chop onion (finely) and add to pan as you cut. Cube tomatoes and add to onion pan.

   Add remaining ingredients and stir. <u>Cover</u>, then turn <u>heat off</u> to let stand.

   ...when timer rings...
   Cook vegetables at med-high. Re-set timer for 5 minutes.

5. <u>Uncover</u> chicken. If there are liquids remaining baste chicken at a higher heat until liquid is gone and chicken is an orange color. <u>Remove from heat</u>. When timer rings for veggies, everything is ready.

Ingredients:

Take out ingredients.

cooking spray (no-cholesterol)
8-12 boneless skinless chicken thighs (approx 800 g)
or skinned drumsticks as shown

1 onion
2 tsp prepared garlic

1 can (284 mL) chicken broth (Campbell's)
2 Tbsp paprika
1 tsp salt
1/2 tsp white pepper

1-1/2 cups white rice (Uncle Ben's Brand)
3 cups water

1 tsp olive oil

1 small onion
2 firm Roma tomatoes

4 cups frozen cut green beans (Green Giant)
2 Tbsp <u>each</u>, of <u>vinegar</u>, <u>soya sauce</u>, <u>ketchup</u> and <u>brown sugar</u>

<u>Serves 4-6</u>

Eating Time

Equipment List:

Lge nonstick fry pan (or electric)
Lge oven-safe pot w/lid
Med nonstick pan w/lid
Can opener
Cutting board
Sharp veggie knife
Lge stirring spoon
Measuring cups & spoons

Per serving:

Calories	428
Fat	8.0 g
Protein	35.6 g
Carbohydrate	53.4 g

Food Choices:

2	Starch
1	Fruit + Veg
0	Milk 1%
1 1/2	Sugars
4 1/2	Protein
1/2	Fat
0	Extras

Prep Time

Paprika Chicken

11

Hogtown Pizza with Salad Greens

Instructions:

Don't change yet! Take out equipment.

1. Preheat oven to 375° F.

    Flatten crust on a cutting surface and cut into 8 triangles. Place on cookie sheet.

    Combine olive oil, garlic and spices in a small cup.

    Remove 1/2 the spiced oil and set aside for salad dressing.

    Brush top of crust with remaining oil.

    Chop green onion.

    Slice artichokes and tomatoes.

    Arrange on crust in this order; green onion, salami, artichokes and tomatoes.

    Sprinkle with grated cheese and bake in **hot oven**. Set timer for 8-12 minutes. Check them at 8 minutes. The edges should be crunchy and a medium brown color.

2. Tear lettuce into bite size pieces into salad spinner and spin dry. **Refrigerate** in spinner.

    Add balsamic vinegar to reserved oil mixture just before serving. Mix well. Serve lettuce on individual dinner plates and drizzle with balsamic dressing.

Ingredients:

Take out ingredients.

1 pkg (283 g) Pillsbury pizza crust

1/3 cup olive oil
2 tsp prepared garlic
1/4 tsp <u>each</u> of <u>dried basil</u>, <u>thyme leaves</u> and <u>rosemary</u>
1/2 tsp oregano leaves

4 green onions

1 can (398mL) artichoke hearts (drained)
you will use 2-3 artichokes
3 firm Roma tomatoes
16 thin slices deli dry salami (approx 50 g)

1 cup grated Gruyere cheese
(low-fat where available)

1 head green leaf lettuce

2 Tbsp balsamic vinegar
croutons (optional)

I slice the artichoke hearts I don't use and freeze them for the next time.

<u>**Serves 4-6**</u>

Eating Time

Equipment List:

Cookie sheet w/edges
Salad spinner
Small bowl or cup
Cheese grater
Cutting board
Sharp veggie knife
Sharp knife
Can opener
Pastry brush
Measuring cups & spoons

Per serving:

Calories	374
Fat	21.9 g
Protein	13.2 g
Carbohydrate	30.8 g

Food Choices:

1 1/2	Starch
1/2	Fruit + Veg
0	Milk 1%
0	Sugars
1 1/2	Protein
4	Fat
0	Extras

Prep Time

Hogtown Pizza

11

Things You Should Know About the Recipes

Red Wings
When we have this as a meal, let me tell you, no one goes anywhere. Note...you must wait until the pastry is a med-dark golden brown before taking them out of the oven. Make sure they have lots of space between them on the pan.

Yellow Wings
I boil my meatballs for two reasons. The oil will rise to the top and drain off with the water. Ground meats usually take a long time to reach a safe 160° F temperature to kill the bacteria, which usually leaves a meatball dry. When you boil them they are soooo moist. Our test families tell us they will never fry them again!

Blue
This is totally gourmet. Some test families tell me they like the cranberries, some think the blueberries are the way to go. Either way, this is an amazing supper.

Red Wings
It's delicious, it's fast and it's fabulous with soya hamburger replacement.

Green
Last but not least!!! The last recipe! It's kinda weird! I've been working so long on this Cookbook! All these years..and here it is ...the last recipe! You would like to get to the food, wouldn't you?

This is such a delicious supper. It's sooo easy! This is not only a family hit but also is fantastic for entertaining! Check out the illustration... For me...this is what supper is all about!

Week 12

Red Wings: Baked Brie with Strawberry Sauce
and Fresh Fruit

Our family rating: 9
Your family rating: _____

Yellow Wings: Honey-Garlic Meatballs with Rice,
Broccoli and Corn

Our family rating: 9
Your family rating: _____

Blue: Stuffed Chicken Breasts with Berry Sauce,
Roasted Potatoes and Corn

Our family rating: 9
Your family rating: _____

Red Wings: Lean Harvest Chili with Cheddar Biscuits

Our family rating 9
Your family rating_____

Green: Italian Baked Chicken with Garlic Fusilli
and Vegetables

Our Family Rating: 10
Your Family Rating: _____

12

Baked Brie with Strawberry Sauce and Fresh Fruit

Instructions:

Don't change yet! Take out equipment.

1. Preheat oven to 375° F.

   Place the white of an egg in a cup.

   Unroll pastry from package. Seal the perforated edges to make two large rectangles. Cut each of those in 1/2 and stretch to make 4 squares of pastry.

   Cut the Brie rounds in 1/2. Place each half on centre of each pastry square.

   Pick up opposite corners of the square and pinch pastry together from peak down both sides. Make sure it's sealed well. Let the peak fall to the side.

   Pick up the two remaining ends and tie them in a loose knot letting the ends of the knot fall to opposite sides of the bundle.

   Brush the bundle with egg white and place a few slivered almonds on top.

   Place bundles on an <u>ungreased</u> cookie sheet leaving lots of space between them to puff up. Bake in **hot oven**. Set timer for 20 minutes or until they are a deep golden brown.

   Mix jam with wine and water in a small container. Set aside.

2. Cut cantaloupe into 1" thick slices, removing seeds. Wash grapes and strawberries.

3. Serve the Brie on individual serving plates. Drizzle the wine sauce all around them directly onto the plate. Serve beside fruit. Nuuuum!!!

Ingredients:

Take out ingredients.

1 egg

1 pkg (318 g) Pillsbury Jumbo Crescents

2 pkg (125 g each) Brie cheese rounds

It may not look pretty yet, but when it's baked you're going to be veeery impressed with yourself.

1 Tbsp slivered almonds (optional)

8 Tbsp 3 fruit jam (strawberry or raspberry)
2 Tbsp each of <u>red wine</u> and <u>water</u>

1 small cantaloupe (approx 500 g)
1 lge bunch green grapes (approx 450 g)
8 fresh strawberries

If it's winter and I can't get strawberries, I scatter some frozen blueberries in for colour. They only take a few minutes to defrost.

<u>**Serves 4**</u>

Eating Time

164

Equipment List:

Cookie sheet w/edges
Colander
Small bowl
Small cup
Cutting Board
Sharp knife
Sharp veggie knife
Pastry brush
Small mixing spoon
Measuring spoons

Per serving:

Calories	566
Fat	24.9 g
Protein	17.2 g
Carbohydrate	68.5 g

Food Choices:

1	Starch
2 1/2	Fruit + Veg
0	Milk 1%
3	Sugars
2	Protein
3 1/2	Fat
0	Extras

Prep Time

Baked Brie

Honey-Garlic Meatballs with Rice, Broccoli & Corn

Instructions:

Don't change yet! Take out equipment.

1. Fill a large **stove-top** pot with water. <u>Cover</u> and bring to a boil.

2. Rinse vegetables under cold water in a colander. Combine with a small amount of water in a small **stove-top** pot. Let stand.

3. Shape meatballs tightly and drop into **boiling water** as you shape. Set timer for 7 minutes after the last meatball has been dropped into the water. (Make sure the water comes to a full rolling boil.)

4. Combine rice and water in a large microwave-safe pot or casserole dish with lid. <u>Cover</u> and **microwave** at high. Set timer for 20-25 minutes.

5. Turn on the heat for your vegetables now at med-low.

6. Drain water from meatball pot when the meat is fully cooked. Return pot to stove and pour sauce over meatballs. Cook at med-high <u>uncovered</u>, stirring as often as you can, until rice timer rings and rice has set for 5 minutes.

7. Add pepper to vegetables and butter if you must.

    <u>Stir and simmer until rice is done.</u>

Remember to stir your meatballs often so they are being entrenched with the sauce. When doing your rice in the microwave you should let it stand about 5 minutes after cooking...about the time it takes to set the table.

Ingredients:

Take out ingredients.

6 L of water (approx)

2 cups frozen cut broccoli (Green Giant)
2 cups frozen Peaches & Cream corn (Green Giant)

675 g ground beef (90% lean)

1-1/2 cups white rice (Uncle Ben's Brand)
3 cups water

1 jar (341 mL) V-H honey-garlic sauce (for spareribs)

fresh ground pepper to taste
butter or margarine (optional)

<u>Serves 4-6</u>

Eating Time

Equipment List:

Lge stove-top pot w/lid
Lge microwave-safe pot w/lid
Small stove-top pot
Colander
Lge mixing spoon
Measuring cups and spoons

Per serving:

Calories	611
Fat	17.6 g
Protein	27.6 g
Carbohydrate	85.6 g

Food Choices:

3	Starch
0	Fruit + Veg
0	Milk 1%
4	Sugars
3	Protein
2	Fat
0	Extras

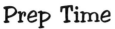

Prep Time

Honey-Garlic Meatballs

12

Stuffed Chicken Breasts with Berry Sauce
Roasted Potatoes and Corn

Instructions:

Don't change yet! Take out equipment.

1. Preheat oven to 350° F.

2. Heat berries and sugar in a small **stove-top** pot on medium.

   Combine in this order, in a small cup; cornstarch, gradually stir in water, lemon juice and spice.

   Stir until smooth and add mixture to berries. Stir until bubbly and slightly thickened, then <u>remove from heat and let stand</u>.

3. Place potatoes in an <u>oven-safe</u> baking dish or pan. Drizzle with a small amount of oil, then toss and sprinkle with spices.
   Bake in **hot oven**.

4. Combine contents according to package directions in a **stove-top** pot. *We omit the butter.* Add brown sugar to the pot. Stir, <u>cover</u> and **remove from heat**.

   Spray a large cake pan or baking dish with cooking spray and make eight mounds of stuffing on the pan.

   Cut each chicken breast <u>in half</u>. Place one piece of chicken on each mound of stuffing and sprinkle the tops with spices. Cover with corn flake crumbs and place in **hot oven** beside the potatoes. Set timer for 45 minutes.

5. Rinse vegetables in colander under cold water. Place in a small microwave-safe pot or casserole dish <u>with lid</u>. **Microwave** at high for 5 minutes, then let stand.

   Microwave corn for 2 additional minutes <u>just before serving</u>. Add salt and butter if you must.

Ingredients:

Take out ingredients.

300 g frozen unsweetened blueberries or cranberries
1/4 cup sugar

1 tsp cornstarch
1/4 cup water
1 Tbsp lemon juice (if using blueberries)
1/4 tsp cinnamon

2 cans (398 mL each) whole potatoes (drained)
1/2 Tbsp canola or olive oil
1/2 tsp each of <u>paprika</u>,
<u>**Italian seasoning**</u> **and** <u>**fresh pepper**</u>

1 pkg (120 g) Uncle Ben's Stuff'N Such
Traditional Sage
1 Tbsp brown sugar

cooking spray (no cholesterol)

4 large boneless skinless chicken breasts (approx 700 g)
fresh ground pepper to taste
1 tsp Mrs. Dash Original Seasoning
2/3 cup corn flake crumbs (approx)

3 cups frozen Peaches & Cream corn (Green Giant)

pinch of salt (optional)
butter or margarine (optional)

<u>Serves 4-6</u>

Eating Time

Equipment List:

2 rectangular cake pans
Med stove-top pot
Small microwave-safe pot w/lid
Small stove-top pot
Colander
Small cup
Cutting board
Sharp meat knife
Can opener
Small & lge mixing spoons
Measuring cups and spoons

Per serving:

Calories	442
Fat	4.2 g
Protein	33.7 g
Carbohydrate	67.5 g

Food Choices:

3 1/2	Starch
1/2	Fruit + Veg
0	Milk 1%
1	Sugars
4	Protein
1/2	Fat
0	Extras

20

Prep Time

Stuffed Chicken Breasts

12

Lean Harvest Chili with Cheddar Biscuits

Instructions:

Don't change yet! Take out equipment.

1. Preheat oven to 450° F.

2. Brown meat in a large, deep **stove-top** pot at med-high until meat is no longer pink.
Putting a lid on the pot speeds up the cooking time.

Add spices to pot.

...while meat is browning...

3. Combine biscuit mix, milk and cheese, in that order, in a mixing bowl. Stir hard with a fork until well combined.

Spoon this mixture onto a well floured surface and knead until no longer sticky. Roll out to a circle, about 1/2" thick, with a rolling pin or wine bottle. Slice into 8 triangles.

Spray a cookie sheet with cooking spray and place triangles on the cookie sheet. Bake in **hot oven**. Set timer for 8 minutes or until biscuits are a light golden brown.

4. Add to **cooked meat** in this order; soup (stir), tomatoes, beans and mushrooms. Stir well. Bring to a boil, <u>reduce heat</u> and simmer. Set timer for 20 minutes.

When the biscuits have finished baking, just let them cool in a beautiful basket on the table until the chili is ready. The family will think you've lost it!!

Ingredients:

Take out ingredients.

675 g ground beef (90% lean)

1 Tbsp <u>each</u> of <u>chili powder</u> and <u>cumin</u>
1/8 tsp cayenne pepper

2 cups biscuit mix
2/3 cup 1% milk (or follow pkg directions)
1/2 cup grated low-fat Cheddar cheese

flour

cooking spray (no-cholesterol)

1 can (284 mL) tomato soup (Campbell's)
1 can (398 mL) chili stewed tomatoes
1 can (398 mL) brown beans in sweet sauce
1 can (398 mL) red kidney beans
1 can (284 mL) sliced mushrooms (drained)

<u>Serves 4-6</u>

Eating Time

Equipment List:

Cookie sheet w/edges
Lge stove-top pot w/lid
Mixing bowl
Rolling pin (or wine bottle)
Can opener
Fork
Lge mixing spoon
Measuring cups & spoons

Per serving:

Calories	624
Fat	25.9 g
Protein	37.2 g
Carbohydrate	60.5 g

Food Choices:

2 1/2	Starch
1	Fruit + Veg
0	Milk 1%
1 1/2	Sugars
4 1/2	Protein
3	Fat
0	Extras

Prep Time

Lean Harvest Chili

Italian Baked Chicken with Garlic Fusilli and Vegetables

Instructions:

Don't change yet! Take out equipment.

1. Set oven to 375° F.

   Place chicken in a large oven-safe cake pan or casserole dish.

   Sprinkle with rosemary.

   Sprinkle with brown sugar.

   Drain mushrooms and scatter sliced mushrooms over each thigh.

   Cover each thigh with sauce one spoon at a time and place in **hot oven** <u>uncovered</u>. Set timer for 40 minutes.

2. Rinse vegetables in colander under cold water. Place in a microwave-safe pot or casserole dish with lid. Sprinkle with spices and toss with soya sauce. <u>Cover</u> and **microwave** at high for 5 minutes, then let stand.

3. Fill a large **stove-top** pot with water. <u>Let stand</u>.

   When the timer rings for the chicken, **leave it in the oven** and bring water to a boil.

   Add pasta to the boiling water. Set timer for 7 minutes. Stir occasionally.

   Rinse pasta in a colander under hot water when the timer rings. Return to pot <u>no heat</u> and toss with a little olive oil if you wish.

4. **Microwave** vegetables at high for 2 additional minutes <u>just before serving</u>.

Ingredients:

Take out ingredients.

8-12 boneless skinless chicken thighs (approx 800 g)

1 tsp dried rosemary <u>for all</u> (not ground)

1 tsp brown sugar <u>per thigh</u>

1 can (284 mL) sliced mushrooms (drained)

1 jar (700 mL) Catelli Garden Select pasta sauce *Parmesan & Romano*

1 pkg (500 g) Green Giant Japanese Style frozen vegetables
1 tsp Mrs. Dash Original Seasoning
1/8 tsp basil
1 Tbsp soya sauce

6 L water (approx)

1 pkg (375 g) Catelli Bistro fusilli pasta *Garlic & Parsley*

1 tsp olive oil (optional)

<u>Serves 4-6</u>

60

Eating Time

Equipment List:

Lge cake pan or casserole dish
Lge stove-top pot w/lid
Microwave-safe pot w/lid
Colander
Can opener
Small mixing spoon
Measuring spoons

Per serving:

Calories	524
Fat	9.7 g
Protein	39.6 g
Carbohydrate	69.7 g

Food Choices:

3	Starch
1 1/2	Fruits + Veg
0	Milk 1%
1	Sugars
4 1/2	Protein
1/2	Fat
0	Extras

Prep Time

Supper Time

Italian Baked Chicken

Favorites

Write in your own family favorites writing left to right (the fastest way to read a recipe when you're in a rush)

Colour

Use a pencil crayon to colour in the cook and prep symbols for easy reference

Component

Incorporate all the components to finish your recipe (rice, pasta, etc.) and put in your own component symbols to the left

MY RECIPES

Write your own recipe reading left to right.

Prep
Time

_____

Instructions:

Don't change yet! Take out equipment.

Ingredients:

Take out ingredients.

Eating Time

Write your own recipe reading left to right.

Prep Time

_____

Instructions:

Don't change yet! Take out equipment.

Ingredients:

Take out ingredients.

Eating Time

Write your own recipe reading left to right.

Prep Time

_____

Instructions:

Don't change yet! Take out equipment.

Ingredients:

Take out ingredients.

Eating Time

Write your own recipe reading left to right.

Instructions:

Don't change yet! Take out equipment.

Ingredients:

Take out ingredients.

Eating Time

Write your own recipe reading left to right.

_____

Instructions:

Don't change yet! Take out equipment.

Ingredients:

Take out ingredients.

Eating Time

Write your own recipe reading left to right.

Instructions:

Don't change yet! Take out equipment.

Ingredients:

Take out ingredients.

Eating Time

Write your own recipe reading left to right.

Prep Time

_____

Instructions:

Don't change yet! Take out equipment.

Ingredients:

Take out ingredients.

Eating Time

Write your own recipe reading left to right.

_____

Instructions:

Don't change yet! Take out equipment.

Ingredients:

Take out ingredients.

Eating Time

Write your own recipe reading left to right.

Prep Time

_____

Instructions:

Don't change yet! Take out equipment.

Ingredients:

Take out ingredients.

Eating Time

Conversion Chart

Monitoring Your Fat (for the day)

Percent	If You Eat	Your Daily Fat Intake Should Be
30%	1500 calories	50 grams
	2000 calories	67 grams
	2500 calories	83 grams
	3000 calories	100 grams
25%	1500 calories	42 grams
	2000 calories	56 grams
	2500 calories	69 grams
	3000 calories	83 grams
20%	1500 calories	33 grams
	2000 calories	44 grams
	2500 calories	56 grams
	3000 calories	67 grams

Oven Temperatures

°F		°C	°F		°C
175	-	80	350	-	175
200	-	95	375	-	190
225	-	110	400	-	205
250	-	120	425	-	220
275	-	140	450	-	230
300	-	150	475	-	240
325	-	160	500	-	260

What We Say and What We Mean

Rectangular lasagna or cake pan means
Approx 9"x13" pan with sides.

Square baking pan means
Approx 8"x8" or 9"x9" pan with sides.

Cookie sheet means
Large pan with short edges.

Broiler pan means
The pan that comes with your stove. It is large, and has a slotted cooking surface which fits over a bottom pan to catch drippings.

Colander means
A large bowl with holes to drain pasta or rinse vegetables in the sink.

GROCERY LISTS

Tear these grocery lists
out of the book or photocopy
them and store them in
the back pocket.

Choose your favorite meals and
customize your own lists.

It's all ready for you.

Custom Grocery List

Recipe Name   Page #

_____

_____

_____

_____

_____

Meats

Dairy

Produce

Dry Essentials

Spices

Baking Goods

Helpers

Frozen Food

Bakery

Other

Meats

8-12 chicken thighs boneless skinless
   (approx 800 g)
1.350 kg 90% lean ground beef (for 2 meals)
3 chicken breasts boneless skinless (approx 450 g)
8 med thickness pork chops boneless & trimmed
   (approx 700 g)

Dairy

butter or margarine
1% milk
100 g low-fat Cheddar cheese (1 cup grated)
100 g part-skim mozzarella cheese (1 cup grated)
fat-free sour cream (optional)

Produce

4 small onions *or 2 large*
1/2 red pepper *or 1 small*
1/2 green pepper *or 1 small*
2 green onions
4 Roma tomatoes
2 avocados
20 mushrooms
1 small zucchini
prepared garlic (in a jar)

Dry Essentials

1-1/2 cups white rice (Uncle Ben's Brand)
350 g spaghettini pasta (Catelli)
1-1/2 cups instant potato flakes (McCain)
1 pkg (375 g) Catelli Express Oven Ready lasagna
   noodles (12)
1-1/2 cups Basmati rice (Uncle Ben's Brand)

Bakery

1 loaf unsliced focaccia *or multigrain bread*
   (optional)

Extras

Spices

salt & black pepper
lemon pepper
cayenne pepper
crushed chilies
curry powder
garlic powder
basil leaves
rosemary leaves
ground cinnamon
Mrs. Dash Original Seasoning

Baking Goods

brown sugar
canola and extra virgin olive oils
cornstarch

Helpers

ketchup
1-1/4 cups chunky salsa
1/3 cup V-H honey-garlic sauce
1 can (284 mL) chicken broth (Campbell's)
prepared mustard
1 can (284 mL) cream of mushroom soup
   (Campbell's)
Worcestershire sauce
1 can (127 mL) chopped green chilies (Old El Paso)
1 can (284 mL) Cheddar cheese soup (Campbell's)
soya sauce
liquid honey

Frozen Food

1 pkg (500 g) California Style vegetables
   (Green Giant)
1 pkg (500 g) baby carrots (Green Giant)
1 pkg (500 g) mixed vegetables (Green Giant)

Custom Grocery List

Recipe Name   Page #

_____
_____
_____
_____
_____

Meats

Dairy

Produce

Dry Essentials

Spices

Baking Goods

Helpers

Frozen Food

Bakery

Other

Meats

900 g 90% lean ground beef
8-12 pork chops boneless & trimmed
  (approx 700 g)
3 chicken breasts boneless skinless (approx 450 g)
450 g beef sirloin steak boneless & trimmed
450 g cleaned shrimp lge size *or 3 chicken breasts boneless skinless*

Dairy

butter or margarine
1% milk
fat-free sour cream (optional)
1 egg
100 g low-fat Cheddar cheese (1 cup grated)
low-fat grated Parmesan cheese (optional)

Produce

2 celery stalks
1 lge carrot
10 mushrooms
4 green onions
1 small green pepper
1 small red pepper
2 small onions
1 small head lettuce
4 Roma tomatoes
prepared garlic (in a jar)

Dry Essentials

corn flake crumbs (found near coating mixes)
1 pkg (approx 166 g) scalloped potatoes *or cheese potatoes if you prefer*
3 cups white rice (Uncle Ben's Brand)
350 g penne pasta (Catelli)

Other

aluminum foil

Extras

Spices

salt & black pepper
garlic powder
cayenne pepper
Mrs. Dash Original Seasoning
crushed chilies (optional)
paprika
ground ginger
basil leaves
cumin
chili powder

Baking Goods

brown sugar
canola or extra virgin olive oil
cooking spray (no cholesterol)

Helpers

1 pkg large soft tortillas (Old El Paso)
soya sauce
ketchup
Worcestershire sauce
1 can (284 mL) sliced mushrooms
1 can (284 mL) tomato soup (Campbell's)
1-1/2 cups chunky salsa
red wine vinegar
1 can (284 mL) chicken broth (Campbell's)
1 can (284 mL) sliced water chestnuts

Frozen Foods

1 pkg (500 g) Green Giant brussel sprouts
500 g Green Giant French Style green beans
1 pkg (500 g) Green Giant Japanese Style vegetables
1 pkg (approx 200 g) snow peas

Custom Grocery List

Recipe Name   Page #

_____

_____

_____

_____

_____

Meats

Dairy

Produce

Dry Essentials

Spices

Baking Goods

Helpers

Frozen Food

Bakery

Other

Meats

700 g thick beef sausage
4 large chicken breasts boneless skinless
   (approx 700 g)
900 g beef sirloin roast boneless & lean

Dairy

butter or margarine
1-1/4 cups 1% milk
250 mL 1% cottage cheese
low-fat grated Parmesan cheese
200 g part-skim mozzarella cheese (2 cups grated)
50 g low-fat Cheddar cheese (1/2 cup grated)

Produce

3 small to medium zucchini (approx 500 g)
2 heads green leaf or Romaine lettuce
1 apple
2 onions
18 fresh mushrooms
16 new potatoes (approx 1 kg) *or 4 large potatoes*
1 pkg (454 g) baby carrots washed & peeled
2 celery stalks
prepared garlic (in a jar)

Dry Essentials

1 pkg (375 g) Catelli Express Oven Ready lasagna
   noodles (8-12)
corn flake crumbs
375 g linguine (Catelli)
1-1/2 cups white rice (Uncle Ben's Brand)

Bakery

1 French loaf
12 brown to serve soft Italian bread sticks

Extras

Spices

salt & black pepper
garlic powder
thyme leaves
marjoram leaves
bay leaf
parsley flakes
cayenne pepper
crushed chilies
cumin powder

Baking Goods

canola oil and extra virgin olive oils
brown sugar
flour
Bisto Brown Gravy Mix

Helpers

1 jar (700 mL) Catelli Garden Select pasta sauce
   Spicy Onion & Garlic
1 can (284 mL) sliced mushrooms
low-fat Caesar dressing *(or 1 Tbsp strong gourmet
   Caesar + 3 Tbsp lowest-fat mayo)*
1 jar (341mL) V-H dry-garlic sauce (for ribs)
soya sauce
2 cans (284 mL each) mushroom soup
   (Campbell's)
1 can (284 mL) beef broth (Campbell's)
sundried tomato salad dressing
lowest-fat creamy peanut butter

Frozen Foods

2 cups baby carrots (Green Giant)
2 cups cut broccoli (Green Giant)

Other

bamboo skewers

Custom Grocery List

Spices

Baking Goods

Recipe Name   Page #

_____

_____

_____

_____

_____

Helpers

Meats

Dairy

Frozen Food

Produce

Bakery

Dry Essentials

Other

Meats

450 g 90% lean ground beef
4 salmon filets skin removed (approx 800 g) *we use Pink*
3 chicken breasts boneless skinless (approx 450 g)
4 lge chicken breasts boneless skinless (approx 700 g)

Dairy

butter or margarine
1% milk
500 mL 1% cottage cheese
150 g part-skim mozzarella cheese (1-1/2 cups grated)
low-fat grated Parmesan cheese
1 pkg (311 g) Pillsbury bread sticks
1 pkg (340 g) Pillsbury Country Biscuits

Produce

30 mushrooms
2 onions
1 large green pepper *or 2 small*
1 small red pepper
1 small zucchini
1 Roma tomato
1 lemon for salmon (optional)
1 head green leaf lettuce
1 head Romaine lettuce
1 red apple

Dry Essentials

350 g spaghetti (Catelli)
1 pkg (165 g) Uncle Ben's Fast & Fancy *Mushroom* rice
1 pkg (375 g) Catelli Express Oven Ready lasagna noodles (12)
1/2 cup croutons
bread crumbs (fine)
1 pkg (375 g) Catelli Healthy Harvest penne pasta *whole wheat*

Extras

aluminum foil
1 medium size thick paper bag *(or 4 small thin... one inside another x 2)*

Spices

salt & black pepper
lemon pepper
celery salt
ground sage
garlic powder
marjoram leaves
rosemary leaves
thyme leaves
basil leaves
fines herbs
parsley flakes
Mrs. Dash Original Seasoning
curry powder

Baking Goods

canola and extra virgin olive oils
white sugar
cooking spray (no-cholesterol)
flour

Helpers

2 jars (700 mL each) Catelli Garden Select pasta sauce *Spicy Onion and Garlic*
1 jar (700 ml) Catelli Garden Select pasta sauce *Mushrooms & Assorted Peppers*
lowest-fat mayonnaise
dill relish (or hot pepper relish)
low-cal salad dressing
low-fat Caesar dressing *(or 3 Tbsp lowest-fat mayo + 1 Tbsp strong gourmet Caesar)*
1 can (284 mL) cream of mushroom soup (Campbell's)

Frozen Foods

125 g (1 cup) mixed vegetables (Green Giant)
100 g chopped spinach
1 pkg (500 g) cut broccoli (Green Giant)

Bakery

1 French loaf *or baguette*

Custom Grocery List

Recipe Name   Page #

_____

_____

_____

_____

_____

Meats

Dairy

Produce

Dry Essentials

Spices

Baking Goods

Helpers

Frozen Food

Bakery

Other

Meats

4 large pork loin chops boneless and trimmed
   (approx 400 g) *based on 1 chop per person*
3 chicken breasts boneless skinless (approx 450 g)
8-12 chicken thighs boneless skinless
   (approx 800 g) *or drumsticks as shown*
675 g 90% lean ground beef

Dairy

butter or margarine
1% milk
fat-free sour cream

Produce

1 lemon
1 small head broccoli
1 red pepper *or 1/2 large*
1 green pepper *or 1/2 large*
3 small onions
45 mushrooms
1 pkg (454 g) Shanghai noodles
4 nectarines *or 12 apricots* (approx 600 g)
1 bunch green grapes (approx 350 g)
1 small honeydew melon (approx 400 g)
prepared garlic (in a jar)
4 green onions

Dry Essentials

corn flake crumbs (found near chicken coating
   mixes)
1 pkg (approx 166 g) scalloped potatoes *(or cheese)*
1-1/2 cups white or brown rice (Uncle Ben's Brand)

Deli

4 slices black forest ham from deli 1/4"thick
   (approx 160 grams) *This can be replaced with
   smoked chicken or turkey breast.*
4 slices low-fat Swiss cheese (approx 85 g)

Extras

Spices

salt & black pepper
ground ginger
curry powder
basil leaves
rosemary leaves
Mrs. Dash Original Seasoning
nutmeg
garlic powder

Baking Goods

brown sugar
canola oil and extra virgin olive oil
cornstarch
white sugar
flour

Helpers

barbeque sauce *or see back pocket*
1 can (540 mL) whole potatoes
1 can (284 mL) chicken broth (Campbell's)
soya sauce
lowest-fat mayonnaise
lemon juice
real bacon bits (packaged)
ketchup
Worcestershire sauce

Frozen Foods

2 cups baby carrots (Green Giant)
2 cups Peaches & Cream corn (Green Giant)
1 pkg (1 kg) Green Giant Sweetlets peas

Bakery

4 large croissants

Custom Grocery List

Recipe Name   Page #

_____

_____

_____

_____

_____

Meats

Dairy

Produce

Dry Essentials

Spices

Baking Goods

Helpers

Frozen Food

Bakery

Other

Meats

3 chicken breasts boneless skinless (approx 450 g)
4 pork chops 1/2" thick boneless & trimmed
    (approx 400 g) *based on one chop per person*
450 g 90% lean ground beef
1.125 kg beef sirloin steak boneless and trimmed
    for 2 meals

Dairy

butter or margarine
1% milk
1 cup fat-free sour cream
150 g part-skim mozzarella cheese
    (1-1/2 cups grated)
1/2 cup grated low fat Parmesan cheese
50 mL low-fat Cheddar cheese (1 cup grated)

Produce

33 mushrooms
2 onions + 1 small
2 nectarines (150 g each) *or 1 small cantaloupe*
1 small honeydew melon (approx 800 g)
8 strawberries
1 Red Delicious apple
1 head lettuce
3 Roma tomatoes
6 green onions
1 avocado (optional)
2 celery stalks
prepared garlic (in a jar)

Dry Essentials

1 pkg (375 g) Catelli Express Oven Ready lasagna
    noodles (12)
1 bag tortilla chips (Old El Paso)
1 pkg (170 g) Uncle Ben's Classics *Oriental
    Spring Vegetable* rice
1-1/2 cups white or brown rice (Uncle Ben's Brand)

Other

aluminum foil
bamboo skewers

Extras

Spices

salt & black pepper
curry powder
chili powder
celery salt
basil leaves
ground cinnamon
low-sodium vegetable bouillon granules
Mrs. Dash Original Seasoning
Mrs. Dash Italian Seasoning

Baking Goods

canola and extra virgin olive oil
cooking spray (no-cholesterol)
flour
brown sugar

Helpers

2 cups chunky salsa
prepared mustard
ketchup
liquid honey
1 can (398 mL) chili-stewed tomatoes
1 can (398 mL) deep brown beans in sweet sauce
1 can (398 mL) red kidney beans *(or brown beans)*
2 cans (398 mL each) whole potatoes
1 can (341 mL) asparagus *(buy a name brand)*
1 can (284 mL) Cheddar cheese soup (Campbell's)
1 can (284 mL) cream of mushroom soup
    (Campbell's)
Worcestershire sauce
soya sauce
20 black olives (optional)

Frozen Foods

1 pkg (500 g) Green Giant Oriental Style
    vegetables
750 g baby carrots (Green Giant)

Bakery

6 fresh dinner buns

Custom Grocery List

Recipe Name	Page #

Spices

Baking Goods

Meats

Helpers

Dairy

Produce

Frozen Food

Bakery

Dry Essentials

Other

Meats

1.6 kg 90% lean ground beef (for 2 suppers)
3 chicken breasts boneless skinless (approx 450 g)
4 large chicken breasts boneless skinless
    (approx 700 g)
900 g beef sirloin steak boneless & trimmed

Dairy

butter or margarine
1% milk
50 g low-fat Cheddar cheese (1/2 cup grated)
50 g low-fat Swiss cheese (1/2 cup grated)
low-fat grated Parmesan cheese (optional)

Produce

1 small + two medium onions
2 small green peppers
37 mushrooms
2 green onions
4 large potatoes
1 small broccoli floweret
prepared garlic (in a jar)

Dry Essentials

instant mashed potato flakes (McCain)
250 g rotini pasta (Catelli)
350 g linguine pasta (Catelli)
1-1/2 cups Basmati rice (Uncle Ben's Brand)
1 cup bread crumbs

Bakery

8 multigrain buns
8 dinner rolls

Extras

Spices

salt & black pepper
cayenne pepper
crushed chili peppers
cumin powder
curry powder
garlic powder
basil leaves
oregano leaves
celery salt
parsley flakes
Mrs. Dash Original Seasoning
rosemary leaves

Baking Goods

brown sugar
cooking spray (no-cholesterol)
canola & extra virgin olive oils
Bisto Brown Gravy Mix

Helpers

ketchup
Worcestershire sauce
1 cup chunky salsa
1 can (398 mL) Catelli *Mushroom* pasta sauce
2 cans (284 mL each) cream of mushroom soup
    (Campbell's)
2/3 cup teriyaki marinade
lowest-fat mayonnaise
1 can (398 mL) cream style corn (Green Giant)

Frozen Foods

1 pkg (500 g) Peaches & Cream corn
    (Green Giant)
1 pkg (500 g) cut broccoli (Green Giant)
1 pkg (500 g) Green Giant Oriental Style
    vegetables

Custom Grocery List

Recipe Name   Page #

_____

_____

_____

_____

_____

Meats

Dairy

Produce

Dry Essentials

Spices

Baking Goods

Helpers

Frozen Food

Bakery

Other

Meats

1 frying chicken (approx 1.2 kg)
6 chicken breasts boneless skinless (approx 900 g)
450 g sirloin steak boneless & trimmed

Dairy

butter or margarine
1% milk
1-1/3 cup fat-free sour cream
4 eggs
1 pkg (311 g) Pillsbury bread sticks
1 tub (500 mL) 1% cottage cheese
100 g low-fat Monterey Jack cheese (1 cup grated)
100 g low-fat Cheddar cheese (1 cup grated)
150 g part-skim mozzarella cheese (1-1/2 cups grated)
1 cup low-fat grated Parmesan cheese

Produce

4 large potatoes
1 small head lettuce
1 head Romaine lettuce
2 Roma tomatoes
prepared garlic (in a jar)
1 carrot
2 onions
1 zucchini
1 small red pepper
1 small green pepper
7 green onions
10 mushrooms

Dry Essentials

1-1/2 cups white or brown rice (Uncle Ben's Brand)
1 pkg (375 g) Catelli Express Oven-Ready lasagna noodles (12)
1 pkg (375 g) Catelli Bistro fusilli pasta *Garlic & Parsley*
croutons

Extras

Spices

salt & black pepper
crushed chili peppers
ground nutmeg
paprika
basil leaves
rosemary leaves
mint flakes
fines herbs
ground coriander
Mrs. Dash Original Seasoning

Baking Goods

flour
cooking spray (no-cholesterol)
canola and extra virgin olive oils
brown sugar
cornstarch
white sugar

Helpers

1 can (127 mL) green diced chilies (Old El Paso)
lime juice
liquid honey
1 can (284 mL) beef broth (Campbell's)
4 Tbsp black bean sauce
low-cal salad dressing
chili-garlic sauce (*found in ethnic food section*)
chunky salsa (optional)
8 large flour tortillas (Old El Paso)

Frozen Foods

1 pkg (500 g) Peaches & Cream corn (Green Giant)
600 g chopped spinach

Other

hazelnut liqueur
aluminum foil

Custom Grocery List

Recipe Name   Page #
_____
_____
_____
_____
_____

Meats

Dairy

Produce

Dry Essentials

Spices

Baking Goods

Helpers

Frozen Food

Bakery

Other

Meats

450 g 90% lean ground beef
7 chicken breasts boneless skinless (approx 1.05 kg)
1.1 kg beef sirloin steak (boneless & trimmed)

Dairy

butter or margarine
1/2 cup no-fat sour cream
75 g low-fat Cheddar cheese (3/4 cup grated)

Produce

1 onion + 1 small
17 mushrooms
2 small green pepper
1 small red pepper
10 Roma tomatoes
1 small zucchini
1 small head lettuce
4 green onions
1 celery stalk
prepared garlic (in a jar)

Dry Essentials

1 pkg (12) hard taco shells (Old El Paso)
1 pkg (375 g) Catelli Healthy Harvest spaghetti
   whole wheat
3 cups white rice (Uncle Ben's Brand)

Frozen Foods

1 pkg lower-fat deep dish pie crust
500 g French fries (McCain) *or potato nuggets*
1 pkg (500 g) whole green beans (Green Giant)
1 pkg (approx 200 g) frozen snow peas

Extras

Spices

salt & black pepper
cumin powder
chili powder
turmeric
onion flakes
garlic powder
Italian seasoning
thyme leaves
cajun seasoning or seasoning salt (optional)
curry powder

Baking Goods

canola and extra virgin olive oils
brown sugar
cornstarch
cooking spray (no-cholesterol)
1/3 cup cashew nuts (optional)

Helpers

1 can (284 mL) Campbell's Golden Mushroom
   soup
1 can (284 mL) Consomne (Campbell's)
Worcestershire sauce
ketchup
3/4 cup chunky salsa
soya sauce
chili-garlic sauce (*found in ethnic food section*)
1 can (284 mL) chicken broth (Campbell's)
cherry jam
1 cup canned sour cherries with liquids
1/2 cup hot ketchup

Custom Grocery List

Recipe Name   Page #
_____
_____
_____
_____
_____

Meats

Dairy

Produce

Dry Essentials

Spices

Baking Goods

Helpers

Frozen Food

Bakery

Other

Meats

675 g 90% lean ground beef
4 large chicken breasts boneless skinless
   (approx 700 g)
675 g sirloin steak boneless & trimmed
8-12 chicken thighs boneless skinless
   (approx 800 g)
3 chicken breasts boneless skinless (approx 450 g)

Dairy

butter or margarine
1% milk
1 egg
fat-free sour cream
low-fat Cheddar cheese (optional)

Produce

5 green onions
1 small onion
1 small red pepper
1 small papaya
1 head lettuce
15 mushrooms
1 bunch of fresh spinach
prepared garlic (in a jar)
1 small avocado (optional)

Dry Essentials

3 cups white rice (Uncle Ben's Brand)
1 cup corn flake crumbs
croutons *or see back pocket*
1 pkg (350 g) vermicelli pasta (Catelli)
chow mein noodles, dry (optional)
shelled peanuts (optional)

Bakery

6 hamburger buns

Other

1/4 cup sherry *or 1/4 cup red wine w/ 1 Tbsp brown sugar*

Extras

Spices

salt & black pepper
ground cumin
ground ginger
curry powder
tarragon leaves
Mrs. Dash Original Seasoning

Baking Goods

white wine vinegar
cooking spray (no-cholesterol)
canola and extra virgin olive oils
white sugar
cornstarch
brown sugar
dry mustard

Helpers

1 cup teriyaki sauce or marinade
1/4 cup V-H dry-garlic sauce
2 Tbsp tahini *(ground sesame seeds- looks like peanut butter)*
chili-garlic sauce *(found in ethnic food section)*
1/2 cup liquid honey
1 can (398 mL) pineapple slices
prepared mustard
lowest-fat mayonnaise
1 jar (227 mL) V-H plum sauce (optional)
real bacon bits (packaged)
low-cal Italian dressing
1 pkg dry peppercorn sauce (approx 40 g) *usually found near spices*

Frozen Foods

1 pkg (500 g) baby carrots (Green Giant)
1 pkg (500 g) Green Giant Oriental Style vegetables
1 pkg (500 g) cut broccoli (Green Giant)
orange juice

Custom Grocery List

Recipe Name   Page #
_____
_____
_____
_____
_____

Meats

Dairy

Produce

Dry Essentials

Spices

Baking Goods

Helpers

Frozen Food

Bakery

Other

Meats

8 pork chops boneless & trimmed (approx 700 g)
3 chicken breasts boneless skinless (approx 450 g)
8-12 chicken thighs boneless skinless
   (approx 800 g) *or chicken legs as shown*
16 thin sliced dry deli salami (approx 50 g)

Dairy

butter or margarine
1% milk
5 eggs (large)
100 g Gruyere cheese (1 cup grated)
125 g low-fat Cheddar cheese (1-1/2 cups grated)
1 pkg (283 g) Pillsbury pizza crust
low-fat Parmesan cheese (optional)

Produce

3 small onions
6 green onions
1 small green pepper
22 mushrooms
2 heads green leaf lettuce
1 small apple
5 Roma tomatoes
prepared garlic (in a jar)

Dry Essentials

1 pkg (120 g) Uncle Ben's Stuff'N Such
   Traditional Sage
1-1/2 instant potato flakes (McCain)
1-1/2 cups white rice (Uncle Ben's Brand)
croutons (optional) see back pocket
1 pkg (375 g) Catelli Bistro fettuccini pasta
   Italian Herb

Extras

Spices

salt & black pepper
white pepper
curry powder
paprika
basil leaves
thyme leaves
rosemary leaves
oregano leaves
Mrs. Dash Original Seasoning

Baking Goods

brown sugar
canola and extra virgin olive oils
cooking spray (no-cholesterol)
white vinegar
balsamic vinegar

Helpers

1 can (284 mL) cream of mushroom soup
(Campbell's)
Worcestershire sauce
real bacon bits (packaged)
low-cal creamy Italian dressing
3 cups chunky salsa
peach jam
1 can (284 mL) chicken broth (Campbell's)
soya sauce
ketchup
1 can (398 mL) artichoke hearts

Frozen Foods

1 pkg (300 g) mixed vegetables (Green Giant)
1 deep-dish pie crust (lower-fat)
1 pkg (500 g) cut broccoli (Green Giant)
4 cups cut green beans (Green Giant)

Custom Grocery List

Recipe Name   Page #

_____

_____

_____

_____

_____

Meats

Dairy

Produce

Dry Essentials

Spices

Baking Goods

Helpers

Frozen Food

Bakery

Other

Meats

4 large chicken breasts boneless skinless (700 g)
1.350 kg 90% lean ground beef
8-12 boneless skinless chicken thighs (approx 800 g)

Dairy

butter or margarine
1% milk
1 egg
1 pkg (318 g) Pillsbury jumbo crescent rolls
2 rounds (125 g each) Brie cheese
50 g low-fat Cheddar cheese (1/2 cup grated)

Produce

1 small cantaloupe (approx 500 g)
1 large bunch green grapes (approx 450 g)
8 strawberries

Dry Essentials

1-1/2 cups white or brown rice (Uncle Ben's Brand)
2/3 cup corn flake crumbs
tea biscuit mix
1 pkg (120 g) Uncle Ben's Stuff'N Such
  Traditional Sage
1 pkg (375 g) Catelli Bistro fusilli pasta
  Garlic & Parsley

Frozen Foods

1 pkg (500 g) Green Giant Japanese Style
  vegetables
1 pkg (500 g each) cut broccoli (Green Giant)
1 pkg (1 kg) Peaches & Cream corn (Green Giant)
300 g frozen blueberries *or cranberries*

Extras

Spices

salt & black pepper
basil leaves
cayenne pepper
ground cumin
dried rosemary
chili powder
paprika
Italian seasoning
ground cinnamon
Mrs. Dash Original Seasoning

Baking Goods

canola and extra virgin olive oils
cooking spray (no-cholesterol)
brown sugar
white flour
slivered almonds (optional)
white sugar
cornstarch

Helpers

2 cans (398 mL each) whole potatoes
1 jar (700 mL) Catelli Garden Select pasta sauce
  Parmesan & Romano
soya sauce
1 jar (341 mL) V-H honey-garlic sauce (for
  spareribs)
1 can (398 mL) chili-stewed tomatoes
1 can (398 mL) brown beans in molasses
1 can (398 mL) red kidney beans
2 cans (284 mL each) sliced mushrooms
1 can (284 mL) tomato soup (Campbell's)
1/2 cup 3-fruit jam (strawberry)
lemon juice

Other

2 Tbsp red wine (non-alcoholic is great)

We Include
4 Types of Indexes
for Speed

Main Component

chicken, beef, etc.
'cause you have an idea of what
you'd like

Color

for the times when speed is
everything

Alphabetical Listing

'cause you remember the name

Fat Content

from lowest to highest
'cause your health requires you to
watch your fat intake

I
N
D
E
X

Index by Main Component

Beef

Chicken

Chicken (Cont.)

Fish

Pork

Vegetarian

Red Wings	Baked Brie with Strawberry Sauce and Fresh Fruit	164
Yellow	Baked Ham & Swiss with Mushroom Sauce on Croissants and Fresh Fruit (Meat free)	88
Blue	Beef Enchilada Casserole with Tomato-Avocado Salad (Use soya hamburger-substitute)	34
Blue	Cheesy Asparagus-Chicken Lasagna with Fruit Kabobs (Replace chicken with mushrooms and onion)	98
Yellow	Chicken Pot Pie with Green Leaf Salad (Replace chicken with firm tofu)	70
Red Wings	Chicken Primavera with Shanghai Noodles (Replace chicken with extra veggies)	82
Red Wings	Chinese Beef Stir-Fry with Rice (Replace beef with firm tofu or extra veggies)	120
Red Wings	Chunky Chicken Bengalia with Pasta and Vegetables (Replace chicken with firm tofu)	156
Red Wings	Curried Chicken with Linguine and Broccoli (Meat free)	104
Yellow Wings	Hard Shell Tacos with Fixn's (Use soya hamburger-substitute)	130
Yellow Wings	Hazelnut Chicken with Pasta and Salad (Meat free)	124
Yellow Wings	Hogtown Pizza with Salad Greens (Meat free)	160
Yellow Wings	Lean Hamburger Jumble with Buns (Use soya hamburger-substitute)	112
Red Wings	Lean Harvest Chili with Cheddar Biscuits (Use soya hamburger-substitute)	170
Green	Lean Leftover Lasagna with Apple-Caesar Salad and Bread Sticks (Use the leftover soya spaghetti sauce)	76
Red Wings	Lean Mean Taco Salad (Use soya hamburger-substitute)	94
Green	Lean Shepherd's Pie with Multigrain Buns (Use soya hamburger-substitute)	106
Yellow Wings	Lean Sirloin Fajitas with Greens and "The Works" (Replace beef with zucchini)	50
Red Wings	Mushroom Cheddar Soup with Bread Sticks	60
Red Wings	Penne Pasta with Italian Gigi Sauce and Vegetables (Meat free)	48
Blue	Sirloin Pepper Steak Pie with Baked Vegetables (Replace beef with firm tofu)	128
Red Wings	Spaghetti with Lean Spicy Meat Sauce and Garlic Bread (Use soya hamburger-substitute)	68
Yellow	Spicy Stir-Fry Chicken with Rice (Replace chicken with firm tofu)	136
Green	Spinach Lasagna with Bread Rolls	122
Yellow Wings	Szechuan Orange-Ginger Chicken with Pasta and Vegetables (Meat free or replace chicken with firm tofu)	148
Yellow Wings	Teriyaki Chicken Toss with Spaghettini Pasta (Replace chicken with extra veggies)	36
Yellow Wings	Teriyaki Unkabobs with Rice (Replace steak with zucchini)	108
Blue	Zippy Quiche with Tossed Salad (Meat free)	154
Blue	Zucchini Parmesan with Garlic Bread and Salad	56

Index by Color

Red (Cont.)

Yellow

Index by Alphabetical Listing

L M P

Q R S

T Z

Index By Fat Content

10 - 15 Grams

10.15 g	Blue	Stuffed Chicken Breasts with Berry Sauce, Roasted Potatoes and Corn	168
10.18 g	Blue	Cheesy Asparagus-Chicken Lasagna with Fruit Kabobs	98
10.27 g	Blue	Quicky Chicken Florentine with Penne Pasta and Vegetables	72
10.42 g	Yellow Wings	Lean Sirloin Fajitas with Greens and "The Works"	50
11.07 g	Yellow	Chicken Burritos with Salad	118
11.29 g	Red Wings	Salmon Filets with Rice and Mediterranean Vegetables	74
11.77 g	Green	Mushroom Beef with Rice and Vegetables	92
11.79 g	Yellow Wings	Thai Satay with Rice in Lettuce Leaves	64
13.18 g	Red Wings	Mushroom Cheddar Soup with Bread Sticks	60
13.86 g	Blue	Zippy Quiche with Tossed Salad	154
14.03 g	Blue	Zucchini Parmesan with Garlic Bread and Salad	56
14.26 g	Blue	Lavish Stuffed Chicken with Roasted Potatoes and Vegetables	110
14.46 g	Yellow	Right Side Up Stuffed Mushroom Chops with Mashed Potatoes and Veg	152
14.60 g	Blue	Sirloin Pepper Steak Pie with Baked Vegetables	128

15 - 20 Grams

15.15 g	Red Wings	Spaghetti with Lean Spicy Meat Sauce and Garlic Bread	68
15.67 g	Yellow Wings	Lean Hamburger Jumble with Buns	112
17.55 g	Yellow Wings	Honey-Garlic Meatballs with Rice, Broccoli and Corn	166
17.60 g	Green	Lean Leftover Lasagna with Apple-Caesar Salad and Bread Sticks	76
17.78 g	Red	Tangy Meatballs with Rice and Mixed Vegetables	86
18.02 g	Green	Spinach Lasagna with Bread Rolls	122

Over 20 Grams

20.21 g	Green	Lean Shepherd's Pie with Multigrain Buns	106
20.55 g	Red Wings	Lean Mean Taco Salad	94
20.74 g	Blue	Lean Teriyaki Hawaiian Burgers with Papaya Salad	140
21.88 g	Yellow	Baked Ham & Swiss with Mushroom Sauce on Croissants and Fresh Fruit	88
21.94 g	Yellow Wings	Hogtown Pizza with Salad Greens	160
22.17 g	Yellow	Lean Dry-Garlic Beef Sausage with Linguine and Mixed Vegetables	58
23.92 g	Yellow	Lean Meatballs in Mushroom Gravy, Mashed Potatoes and Mixed Veg	40
24.88 g	Red Wings	Baked Brie with Strawberry Sauce and Fresh Fruit	164
25.24 g	Yellow Wings	Hard Shell Tacos with Fixn's	130
25.63 g	Blue	Roast Chicken with Potato Wedges and Corn	116
25.90 g	Red Wings	Lean Harvest Chili with Cheddar Biscuits	170
26.29 g	Blue	Beef Enchilada Casserole with Tomato-Avocado Salad	34
26.45 g	Green	Lean No-Loaf Meatloaf with Scalloped Potatoes and Brussel Sprouts	52

I knew one thing for sure when hiring a photographer for this book, **there would not be a food stylist on our photography shoot**. (You know, the people who use shaving cream and cook things with chemicals so they look appetizing!!) I wanted the food to be...the food! Believe it or not, some photographers refused to take on the job under those conditions but Ian saw this as a challenge. Some photographers feared it would make their work look bad. Ian saw it as a way to show off what he is capable of. This is the best way I can describe Ian Grant. His professional attitude, his immaculate scheduling and his desire to achieve perfection under any circumstance makes his work stand out. There aren't enough thank-yous, Ian!! Bravo!!

Ian Grant Inc. Photography is located in St. Albert, Alberta.

Ian Grant

Judy Schultz

Tannie Hopkins

Lorna Bennett

I have always admired the way Judy was able to write. You could sometimes taste the food by simply reading!! My dream came true when she agreed to be the food editor of our book. I remember my husband and I howling over the introduction of her book <u>Four Seasons</u>. Everything she said was exactly the way our experiences had been with cookbooks! She has a wit that matches ours, she looooves food as much as we do, (I did the looove thing cause it drives her nuts) and she has a journalists eye for error! Judy is the Feature writer for food and travel with the <u>Edmonton Journal</u>, Edmonton, Alberta.

I was so frightened about choosing the right graphic art designer. It needed to be a person who felt like this is their book. I wanted someone to be on time with layout examples and I wanted someone who is flexible (you know, who can check their ego at the door). Wow!! Tannie surpassed any expectation I ever dreamed of. She's a ball of fire and enthusiasm, always on time and a stickler for detail. Lucky us!! Tannie is the owner of "It's Your Thing" Personalized Printing located in Edmonton, Alberta.

Lorna is just plain warped! I warned her I would say that. She somehow managed to find all our true-to-life family chaos hilarious. To see her in action is quite the sight. I will tell her a story, her eyes will light up, she'll jump out of her chair and the next thing I know, there it is, the perfect comic depicting my family. In the process of production and long hours she kept us all howling!! Believe it or not, we did not have a single correction on her comp drawings. Deadlines are not only met, it is kind of her bag!! ...an artsy person who likes deadlines, SEE, I told you she's warped! Thanks, Lorna, and remember I found you first. Lorna is the owner of Lorna Bennett Illustration located in Edmonton, Alberta.

Thank you! Thank you! Thank you!

"I only clean my house spotlessly, for people I don't care for."

I would not clean my house for the following people... For our dear, dear friends that hung in there through thick and thin, through richer and poorer, even when we appeared to disappear from the face of the earth for months at a time! You know who you are....Thanks!! Our beautiful neighbors and friends better known as Jo and Sean's 24 hour on call computer fixing service! (cookies and snacks included) We couldn't have done it without you! To our test families for reluctantly going along with the testing in the first place! ... then for convincing us that no other book in existence is even close to this one. To the more than 120 families who enjoyed our food on a regular basis over the last 3 years. Gail, thanks for being the leader of the band! Dave for your brutal editing and those, "I'm pumped about this book," comments in that fantastic accent! Ramona, we still have the cheque. Thanks for believing at a time when it meant more than you'll ever know! To the Holes. What a beautiful family you are! Lois, if I only become half the person you are, I will have succeeded!! Bill, thanks so much for your time, I will never forget your kindness! To all the people who put their heart and soul into this book! Thanks!

A very warm and heartfelt thanks to Elite Lithographers, Ken, Janet and the crew. Your positive thinking and "Anything can be done, so don't worry" attitude made this such a great experience.

Also, thanks to Alannah and the gang at our local Chapters. They did everything but bring me a latte while I was doing my research. I dubbed it, "The office." Great job ...and abooout that latte?

Our seven children! You always have the ability to keep us laughing! You are the most amazing individuals I have ever been blessed to know!! I know you're all going to call me on the clean house thing, but ....don't get any bright ideas, main chore is still on this week! To the unsung heroes; our oldest son Doug (better known as Oakley Boy) who pumped out up to eighty meals a day in pursuit of perfecting our food. Last but never least; my Project Coordinator. Job description: Purchase or take out every self-publishing book you can get your hands on. ...then read them....all....with coffee, in the washroom, on a trip, in the car driving to the store, in the shower, while sleeping!! He is my Chief Financial Planner, Nutritional Analysis Food Weigher & Inputter, Editor, Editor and Editor, Test Evaluation Consultant, Motivation Consultant & Chief Masseur.......
My beautiful husband and best friend Ron.
Without him there would not be a book! I love you so much!

Glenna, Don, George, we did it, we really did it!! Yahoo!!

P.S. If one of you happens to come over when the house is spotlessly clean, don't panic,..I still love you,.. it will be sheer fluke!

and

WAECHTERSBACH
GERMANY

are
available across
Canada at fine
kitchen stores
and The Bay

A special thanks to Browne & Company for supplying us with all the dishes you see in the photographs. Also, thanks to Le Gnome, Zenari's and Call the Kettle Black in Edmonton for making sure the accessories were perfect!

221

I moan while I eat! I always have!

I was born and raised with my five brothers and sisters in Quebec where food isn't a necessity, it's a part of your culture, your social upbringing and your reason for living!! Ok, so I'm known to exaggerate occasionally. When I remember my childhood I remember food! Like when I was 10 ... my brother Don would con me into helping him collect for his paper route. The lure was egg rolls, the best egg rolls in the world. We would go to the local Chinese restaurant close to our home in Montreal and pig right out!! I know the memory couldn't have been the experience of being with my brother because he was a big turkey!! (I can say that now cause he has since miraculously morphed into a pretty terrific guy!) I remember countless trips to the Cabane à Sucre where everything was plastered in Quebec maple syrup! Ooooor standing at the end of our driveway in St. Agathe smelling the barbeque as I looked down the mountain at the beautiful lake below.

As my love and appreciation of food flourished, I knew that I had to be careful with what I ate. Weight problems were definitely part of my family history. This is what eventually led me to writing this book. You see, ...I never intended to write a book! My passion for food, health and cooking, simply clashed with my "not enough time to cook" life!! As I hunted for a cookbook to solve my dilemma, it became obvious I had better develop my own. The reputation of the recipes grew so fast that they were not only rescuing me, but many others around me!

Look at page 173. This is the way my family and I see supper. Every night we gather, no matter how insane our lives or our schedules are. It's a special time where we connect. No, it's not always peaceful. Yes, they kick and bug each other. Some are grumpy and some are happy. Some got a good mark on their paper and some didn't (but of course they have a perfectly legitimate excuse). We get to talk, laugh, nag and just be a regular old family!! Throughout the years the children have had assignments at school asking them about family traditions. It always chokes me up when one by one, year after year, they all list supper as their most prized family tradition. Though I've helped many others manage the most stressful time of their day, I still get goose bumps each time someone says, "I can't believe how this system has changed the way I see supper!!" Wishing you many moans over dinner!

Sandi Copeman-Richard

222

Website Extras

www.cookingfortherushed.com

- Sandi appears on TV and radio, in newsprint and magazines and at conferences regularly.

- Our Upcoming Events schedule tells when you can see, hear or read about Sandi in your city.

- Conference and workshop information available online.

- Find out about our fundraising opportunity for your nonprofit organization.

Regional Health Management Team

"Please bring her back!"

The Learning Channel

"I'm excited to go home and try what I learned from Sandi."

National News Broadcast

www.cookingfortherushed.com

We would love to hear from you.
Reach us by email at
rsrichard@cookingfortherushed.com

www.cookingfortherushed.com